Alfred Williams Momerie

Church and Creed

Sermons preached in the Chapel of the Foundling Hospital. Second Edition

Alfred Williams Momerie

Church and Creed
Sermons preached in the Chapel of the Foundling Hospital. Second Edition

ISBN/EAN: 9783337173296

Printed in Europe, USA, Canada, Australia, Japan

Cover: Foto ©Lupo / pixelio.de

More available books at **www.hansebooks.com**

Church and Creed

Sermons Preached in the Chapel of the
Foundling Hospital

BY

ALFRED WILLIAMS MOMERIE
M.A., D.SC., LL.D.

LATE FELLOW OF ST JOHN'S COLLEGE, CAMBRIDGE;
PROFESSOR OF LOGIC AND METAPHYSICS
IN KING'S COLLEGE, LONDON

SECOND EDITION

WILLIAM BLACKWOOD AND SONS
EDINBURGH AND LONDON
MDCCCXC

CONTENTS.

	PAGE
THE CHURCH,	1
THE CHURCH OF ENGLAND—	
I. THE CLERGY,	13
II. THE LAITY,	29
THE ATHANASIAN CREED.—I.,	41
THE ATHANASIAN CREED.—II.,	54
SALVATION BY CREED,	70
CHRIST'S PLAN OF SALVATION,	80
THE CONNECTION BETWEEN CREED AND CONDUCT,	92
IDEALS,	105
USE AND ABUSE OF CREEDS,	117
REVERENCE—	
I. ITS DEFINITION,	127
II. THE DIFFERENCE BETWEEN REVERENCE AND RESPECT,	143

REVERENCE: *continued*—

    III. CRITICISMS, . .   157

    IV. ITS EVOLUTION, . . .   169

    V. ITS EVOLUTION—(*continued*), .   182

LITTLE KINDNESSES, .   196

LAUGHTER, .   208

THE RESURRECTION OF THE BODY,   220

THE GODS OF THE BIBLE, . . .   233

THE DIDACHE; OR, TEACHING OF THE TWELVE APOSTLES, . .   246

The Church.

"The general assembly and church of the first-born, who are written in heaven."—HEBREWS xii. 23.

"God is no respecter of persons; but in every nation he that feareth Him, and worketh righteousness, is accepted with Him."—ACTS x. 34, 35.

OUR Ritualistic friends very much dislike to hear the Church spoken of as a sect,—as merely one among a number of opposed and competing denominations. Now I quite agree with them that a Church is, or should be, something essentially different from a sect. But I do not think they generally see in what the true difference consists, nor all that that difference involves.

The etymology of the terms may help us here. It is as a rule desirable, when we wish to find out the best use of words, to inquire into their derivation. We are not obliged, of course, to follow this slavishly; but the study of derivations is always suggestive, and generally speaking the root-meaning of the word is the best. Now church comes from the Greek word κύριος, and means therefore that which belongs to the Lord. Sect is derived from the Latin *sequi*, to follow. A sect consists of those who follow some particular man, as for example Wesleyans, Sandemanians, Swedenborgians, Irvingites; or of those who follow some particular tenet, as for example the Baptists, whose leading doctrine is immersion; or the Independents, whose fundamental principle is that every congregation should manage its own affairs. We shall not be far wrong if we say that the root idea in the word church is God, and the root idea in the word sect is man. It will be worth our while to inquire how far these etymological meanings are borne out in actual fact.

To see this we must first distinguish between *the* Church and *a* Church,—between the Church and Churches. What is meant, or rather what should be meant, by the Church? We were most of us, I suppose, brought up to think that *our* Church was *the* Church,—the English Church if we happened to belong to that, or the Romish Church if we chanced to be Roman Catholics. But a little reflection will show the absurdity, or perhaps I should say the blasphemy, of such a thought. This is very well explained in the last chapter of Mark Pattison's Memoirs, where he describes his deliverance from the thraldom of sectarianism. He was brought up originally in the narrow faith and sympathies of Puritanism. But by-and-by he came to believe in the Anglican Church, and afterwards in the Catholic Church, whose members, united by a common creed, were to be found in all parts of the world. This idea at first filled him with enthusiasm. But even in this broader notion he could not ultimately rest. "The idea of the Catholic Church," he says, "is only a mode of conceiving the dealings of divine Providence with mankind. And reflection gradually convinced me that this theory of the relation of all living beings to the Supreme Being was too narrow and inadequate. It makes an equal Providence, the Father of all, care only for a mere handful of the species, leaving the rest to the chances of eternal misery. If God interferes at all to procure the happiness of mankind, it must be on a far more comprehensive scale than by providing for them a church of which the majority will never hear. It was on this line of thought that I passed out of the Catholic phase to that highest development, in which all religions appear in their historical light as efforts of the human spirit to understand and commune with God." In other words the Catholic Church, which has only existed for two thousand years, which has only been heard of by a small proportion of the race, is not, as its name would imply, universal; and it should be carefully distinguished from what is properly called *the* Church. That must be co-extensive with the race.

And so according to the Bible it is. According to the Bible neither creeds nor rituals have anything to do with membership in the Church of God. The Deity, our text says, cares supremely for goodness—and for goodness alone. "In every nation he that worketh righteousness is accepted." The Church of which he thus becomes a member, though it existed ages before "the Christian era," is not inaptly called the Church of the first-born,—the Church of Christ. "Your father Abraham," said the Saviour, "rejoiced to see my day." My day? Yes. For Christ is but another name for righteousness, of which He was the great example and inspirer. The Church then,—the true Church, the Christian Church, the Church of God, the one eternal and universal Church,—consists of those who are written in heaven because they have worked righteousness on earth. Of this eternal and universal Church, it is manifest, temporary and local churches—such as those of England, of Scotland, even of Rome—can form at the best but parts. They cannot in the nature of things be more.

Well then, you say, what becomes of the distinction between a church and a sect? Does that still hold good? I think it does. I will tell you why. I suppose that the narrowest of the Churches is wider than the broadest of the sects. It is not the holding of certain tenets which makes a sect. For most of the tenets of the sects have been held by members of one or other of the Churches. A sect only arises when persons separate themselves from communion with their Church. It is not the tenets, but isolation on account of the tenets, which constitutes sectarianism. And this isolation shows that an exaggerated and utterly false importance is attached by the schismatics to their own special beliefs. In comparison with righteousness other things are unimportant. And upon the whole I venture to affirm that the Churches of Christendom have come far nearer than the sects to the realisation of this fundamental truth. I don't mean to say, of course, that our dissenting friends are not personally as good as we are. For anything I know to the contrary they may be better. But *as Dissenters* they exist, not to emphasise the importance of righteousness, but to emphasise the importance of something else,—agreement in regard to which is made a *sine quâ non* for membership. Exclusiveness is implied in the very idea of a sect. The Churches may not be sufficiently wide; but the sects are formed on purpose to be narrow.

In common honesty, however, I am bound to admit that the Churches of Christendom, though less narrow than the sects, are far from having attained that breadth of sympathy which should belong to them as parts of the Church of Christ. There is not one of them which has fully realised the divine ideal. The Church of England, it seems to me for reasons which I will hereafter explain, is slowly struggling towards it. In the meantime I would warn you that there are persons *in* your Church but not *of* it, whose chief desire is to degrade it into a sect. At heart they are not Churchmen but Dissenters. Every prosecution for heresy, every prosecution for ritualism, is a deliberate attempt to sectarianise your Church. In all such prosecutions the doctrines and ceremonies of men are made of more importance than the righteousness of God.

The strangest part of it all is that the prosecutors flatter themselves they believe in the teaching of Christ. Yet if Christ were here He would say now, just what He said two thousand years ago; and He would say it with infinite sorrow, that men had not yet learnt the lesson. The disciples, you remember, complained,— "Master, we saw one casting out devils in Thy name, and he followeth not us; and we forbad him, because he followeth not us." But Jesus said, "Forbid him not: for he that is not against us is on our part. Whosoever shall offend one of these little ones that believe in me, it were better for him that a millstone were hanged about his neck, and that he were cast into the sea. It must needs be that offences come, but woe unto that man through whom the offence cometh."

What could be more plain? And yet men are still hankering after uniformity. When will they learn to be content with unity? When will they learn that unity does not involve uniformity,—that the highest unity manifests itself in diversity? The lesson seems a simple one to those who have mastered it. But it is a lesson which was never quickly learned. And here, as elsewhere, the truth is first discovered in the physical sphere. Those who are acquainted with modern science are aware that the infinite variety of Nature is perfectly compatible with her unity. There was a time, however, when unity and diversity were thought to be incompatible. In early ages the world seemed a chaos. Thousands and tens of thousands of conflicting agents were supposed to be at work in the production of natural phenomena. The woods appertained to one set of deities—the dryades; the mountains to another set—the oreades. Every star, every planet, was believed to possess a moving principle peculiar to itself. Storms and earthquakes, pestilences and eclipses, were thought to be the work of a variety of beings, who were guided by all sorts of different motives, and whose future action it was absolutely impossible to predict. The variety in nature prevented men even from imagining the unity of God. The history of science records the gradual discovery in this primeval chaos of the unifying principle of Law. Over and over again, phenomena that seemed altogether dissimilar have turned out to be merely different operations of one and the selfsame force. The apple which falls to the ground once seemed to have nothing in common with the moon which does not so fall. But now we know that both are equally under the control of gravity; that the moon is attracted no less than the apple; and that the tendency to fall earthwards, produced in it by this attraction, is one of the factors determining its course. Whenever we compare phenomena—no matter how distant they may be from each other in time and space, no matter how diverse they may at first sight appear—we now always expect to find in them an underlying unity of thought and purpose and mode of working; and sooner or later our expectations are fulfilled. The infinite variety of nature has been summed up by science in a single word—Evolution.

And what has been done in the sphere of physical science is being accomplished, though more slowly, in the sphere of religion. Here too there is infinite variety,—a variety which at first sight seems quite incompatible with unity. We find worship conducted with the most gorgeous ritual, and we find also worship characterised by the baldest simplicity. We find elaborate liturgies, extempore prayer, and voiceless communion with the Unseen. We find a professed acquaintance with all the purposes of the

Deity, and we find altars erected "to the unknown God." We find men frequenting several times a day the ministry of the clergy, and we find others who declare they are helped more by the ministry of Nature. Yet underlying all this adversity the thinker discovers a single instinct,—the desire to do honour to Him who is regarded as the impersonation of perfect goodness. All these worshippers, differing so much superficially, are nevertheless members one of another; they are all included in "the general assembly and church of the first-born." "In every nation he that worketh righteousness is accepted." The infinite variety of religious thought and observance may all be summed up in that one word—Righteousness.

The Church of Christ is essentially and necessarily a broad church. Broad? That is a poor word. It is wide-reaching as the Infinite. It is a unity; for all its members are bound together by their common love of righteousness. But it admits of infinite diversity. My chief business in life is to explain and enforce this lesson. When men have learned it, there will be no more sects; no more religious, or rather irreligious, persecutions; diversity will remain, but discord will have vanished; all who love righteousness will love one another; religious communities will perceive that they are not separate and antagonistic bodies, but parts of the selfsame organism; and the Churches of the world will become—in a sense quite different from that in which the words can now be applied to them — the Churches of our Lord and of His Christ.

The Church of England.

I.

THE CLERGY.

"*I A. B., do solemnly make the following declaration. I assent to the Thirty-nine Articles of Religion and to the Book of Common Prayer, and of the ordering of bishops, priests and deacons. I believe the doctrine of the united Church of England and Ireland, as therein set forth, to be agreeable to the Word of God; and in public prayer and administration of the sacraments, I will use the form in the said book prescribed, and none other, except so far as shall be ordered by lawful authority.*"—28 & 29 Vict. c. 122.

That is the form of subscription which, since 1865, has been required from beneficed clergymen of the Church of England. The form which had been in use for two centuries previously ran thus: "*I, A. B., do hereby declare my unfeigned assent and consent to all and everything prescribed in and by the book entitled the Book of Common Prayer and Administrations of the Sacraments and other Rites and Ceremonies of the Church according to the use of the Church of England, together with the Psalter or Psalms of David, appointed as they are to be said or sung in churches, and the form or manner of making, ordering and consecrating of bishops, priests, and deacons.*"

The change to which I wish to-day specially to call your attention is this: instead of "unfeigned assent and consent to all and everything contained in the Book of Common Prayer," which was required in 1662, there was substituted in 1865 a declaration of belief, that "the doctrine of the Church of England as contained in the Prayer-book is not contrary to the Word of God." I am going to explain to you the meaning of this change, and the various considerations which led to it.

There had long been a growing dissatisfaction with the stringency of the old form of subscription. In 1862 a letter on the subject was addressed by Stanley to Dr Tait, then Bishop of London; and in this letter the evils of the system were clearly and powerfully exposed. Stanley began by giving a brief summary of the history of subscription. The three first centuries of the Christian Church were entirely without it. The members of the Church made a profession of their faith at baptism; but this was in the simplest form. It was not an assent to a variety of intellectual propositions, but a profession of service under a new master and of entrance into a new life. No deacon, no presbyter, no bishop made any subsequent profession. The distinction between the requirements of belief from clergy and laity was as yet wholly unknown.

The first subscription to a confession of faith was that enforced by Constantine at the Council of Nicea. "It was the natural but rude expedient of a half educated soldier to enforce unanimity in the Church, as he had by the sword enforced it in the Empire." Subscription, however, was only demanded from the bishops, not from the clergy generally. And it seems to have been accompanied by the same casuistry, the same ambiguity, and the same inoperative results then as now.

The Reformed Churches on the Continent, in order to protect themselves from the enemies that hemmed them in or were supposed to hem them in on every side, constructed the most elaborate and stringent Confessions of Faith. In the Duchy of Brunswick, for example, Duke Julius required from all clergy, from all professors, from all magistrates, a subscription to all and everything contained in the Confession of Augsburg, in the Apology for the Confession, in the Smalcaldic Articles, in all the works of Luther, in all the works of Melanchthon, and in all the works of Chemnitz. But this excess of subscription was followed—not unnaturally—by its entire or almost entire extinction.

In England, Stanley showed, subscriptions had been gradual, capricious and accidental growths. Our Church as such recognises absolutely no subscriptions. "They have grown up as a mere excrescence, through the pressure of political and ecclesiastical parties." The Articles were not subscribed by anything like general usage till the twelfth year of Elizabeth. They were then, after much hesitation and opposition, ordered to be subscribed for a special purpose, and with a limitation which considerably mitigated the evil it introduced. The purpose was to check the admission of Presbyterian ministers into the Church of England without re-ordination. And the limitation consisted in the fact that the clergy were to subscribe only those Articles which concern the "confession of the true faith and the doctrine of the sacraments." The liturgy was not subscribed till the reign of James I. "Then, by a paradox unknown to any other Church in Christendom, the liturgy was turned from its proper purpose of expressing the devotion of the congregation, into a storehouse of theological propositions, to be enforced on all those who had not the knowledge to distinguish between the nature of a liturgy and a creed." Finally, by the Act of Uniformity passed under Charles II., the stringency of subscription to both Articles and liturgy was increased, with the express purpose of driving from their places in the Church as many of the Puritan clergy as possible. Unfeigned assent and consent to all and everything contained in the Prayer-book was then demanded from every clergyman of the Established Church.

This demand—which was still made in 1862, the date of Stanley's letter—was at once absurd, mischievous and futile.

I. It was absurd. For the Articles consist of a number of complicated propositions drawn up by men who lived three hundred years ago, in the heat of vehement struggles which have long since passed away—" by men who, venerable as they were in station, and some of them estimable in character and distinguished in ability and learning, were still not the foremost men of the age in which they lived, and therefore not the men whose expressions on these subjects we should most naturally expect to be permanent." It might be said that the evil of subscription was diminished by the liturgy; since there is hardly a statement in the Articles to which objection can be raised, that is not neutralised by some countervailing expression in the liturgy. But manifestly the fact that the one may be corrected by the other is no reason for giving unfeigned assent and consent to all and everything contained in both. As some parts of the Prayer-book are inconsistent with other parts in spirit if not in form, to demand assent to everything contained in it is to ask for the impossible,—which is absurd.

II. Sometimes the absurdity was not seen, and then the demand led to many mischievous consequences. It was often thought that the terms of subscription must be understood in their most rigid sense, and that every word in the Prayer-book must be accepted, without regard to the general spirit of the whole. Many devout and earnest students were on this ground prevented from taking orders, and their services were thus lost to the Church. Intelligent and thoughtful men " could not assent to the literal and dogmatic meaning of the six hundred propositions on the most intricate and complex subjects which the

Articles embody; they could not assent to the literal and dogmatic meaning of all the sentences in the liturgy,—many of them poetical and devotional in form, but which must be received, according to a strict subscription, in their most prosaic and matter-of-fact signification; still less could they assent with unhesitating confidence to both these sets of propositions, emanating from ages unlike each other, and each no less unlike our own." All, therefore, who thought that the Church required this of them, had nothing for it but to remain outside.

But the worst mischief caused by subscription was within the Church itself. The Articles and the liturgy were turned into weapons of recrimination. In times of controversy "no phrase of the Articles was too parenthetical, no term of the liturgy too rhetorical, to be pressed into the service." The large and liberal constructions which were generally admitted in times of peace, and which every party in the Church was obliged to claim for its own interpretation, were—when used by theological opponents—branded as sophistry or disingenuous subtlety. To the general evils of controversy were thus added the great and peculiar aggravation of the embitterment caused by mutual imputations of dishonesty and bad faith. We need only recall the language employed by High Churchmen against Low Churchmen in the Gorham controversy, by Low Churchmen against High Churchmen in the controversy of the 'Tracts for the Times;' and by the extreme partisans of both these sections in the controversy of the 'Essays and Reviews.' All such exhibitions of internecine warfare caused great scandal, and brought the Church into contempt.

III. And where subscription was not mischievous, it was at all events futile. It did not produce uniformity. Those who subscribed were obliged, in the nature of things, to give to the Articles and liturgy a more or less liberal interpretation. They felt that the mere fact of the enormous scope of the subscription, involving assent to documents so various in kind and in part so contradictory, must by the very force of the terms imply a general and not a particular assent—a reception of the whole, not a reception of each particular part. The Low Churchman interpreted the Liturgy by the Articles; the High Churchman interpreted the Articles by the Liturgy; the Broad Churchman adopted what he conceived to be the general spirit of both.

Stanley gave many illustrations of the fact, that those who had subscribed according to the old form, nevertheless did not accept "all and everything contained in the Prayer-book." According to the Athanasian Creed, for example, every single member of the Greek Church must "perish everlastingly," because he does not believe that the Holy Ghost proceeds from the Father *and the Son*. But an eminent prelate once said—"I never met with a single clergyman who believed this in the literal sense of the words; and for the honour of human nature and of Christianity, I trust not one lives who would deliberately aver that such was his belief." The doctrine, therefore, which the Creed condemns was thus generally admitted within the pale of the English Church.

Again, the sixth Article " understands by Holy

Scripture those canonical books of the Old and New Testament of whose authority was never any doubt in the Church." Taken literally, the subscription to these words would exclude from the clerical profession all those who receive as Holy Scripture the Epistle to the Hebrews, the Apocalypse, the second Epistle of St Peter, the Epistles of St James and St Jude, and the second and third Epistles of St John,—of whose authority it is well known there was considerable doubt in the early Church. "Yet this statement of the Article was not only overridden but even forgotten; and the vast majority of the clergy of the Church of England, in defiance of the Article and of their subscription to it, received as Holy Scripture without scruple those books of whose authority there was doubt in the Church for no less than three important centuries; and they even attacked as heretical those who adopted the language of the Article itself."

Illustrations of this kind may be multiplied indefinitely. "If once," said Stanley, "we press the subscriptions in their rigid and literal sense, it may safely be asserted there is not one clergyman in the Church who can venture to cast a stone at another; they must all go out, from the Primates at Lambeth and Bishopsthorpe to the humblest curates of Wales or Westmoreland."

The continued existence of the Church of England, therefore, depended upon a wide latitude in the interpretation of the Prayer-book. Every clergyman allowed himself more or less liberty, as to what he accepted and in what sense he accepted it. But with this latitude the old form of subscription was on the face of it inconsistent. "Assent to all and everything" in the Prayer-book was a very bad form of words for expressing assent to the general tenor of it. And this manifest inconsistency, between the supposed requirements of subscription and what happened in actual fact, led frequently to much bitter recrimination, and to the exclusion from the ministry of many whose services would have been most valuable to the Church.

On these grounds, therefore, Stanley prayed the Bishop of London, the rest of the episcopate, and the legislature in general, to take the whole question of subscription into their serious consideration. "It was observed," he said in conclusion, "of the oracle of Delphi, that during all the ages in which it commanded the real reverence of Greece, the place in which it was enshrined needed no walls for its defence. The awful grandeur of its natural situation, the majesty of its temple, were sufficient. Its fortifications, as useless as they were unseemly, were built only in that disastrous time when the ancient faith had decayed, and the oracle was forced to rely upon the arm of flesh, on its bulwarks of brick and stone, not on its own intrinsic sanctity. May God avert from us this omen! It is only in these later ages of the Church, and chiefly in the Protestant portions of Christendom, that subscriptions have been piled up to circumscribe our oracle and sanctuary. Let us show that we, in these later days, are willing to free ourselves from such unsightly barriers, which encumber, without defending, the truth that they enclose and hide. Let us show that we in our Reformed Church are not afraid to dispense with those artificial restraints, which the Catholic Church, in ancient and as we think less enlightened times, scorned to call to its aid."

In the following year, 1863, mainly I suppose owing to Stanley's letter, a Royal Commission was issued for the purpose of examining fully into the subject. The result of their inquiry was the introduction of a Bill by Lord Granville in 1865, in which the old, precise, stringent form of subscription was completely set aside, and another declaration was substituted for it — that which I read as my text — a declaration as bare and general as it was possible to be, consistently with the retention of any expression of assent at all.

And I cannot too strongly impress upon you the fact that this change was made distinctly for the purpose of broadening the Church. Mr Buxton, in his speech before the House of Commons, said—" It was the express intention of the Commission to relax the extravagant stringency of the existing tests; in other words, to make it possible for men to minister at the altars of the Church, though they might dissent from some part of her teaching. . . . All those phrases which indicated that the subscriber declared his acceptance of every dogma of the Church had been swept away; and this had been done expressly and of forethought. Instead of declaring his assent to all and everything the Prayer-book contained, a clergyman now only declared his assent to the Prayer-book itself, that is to say to the book as a whole, and his belief that the doctrine of the Church therein set forth was agreeable to the Word of God. He would not declare that the doctrines in the plural number, or that each and all of the doctrines, were agreeable to the Word of God, but only the doctrine. It was expressly and unanimously agreed by the Commission that the word doctrine should be used in the singular number, in order that it might be understood that it was the general teaching, and not every part and parcel of that teaching, to which assent was given." After its scope and purpose had been thus distinctly explained to them, the Bill was passed by both Houses of Parliament, and it is now the law of the land.

The next time therefore you are asked, as

foolish people are so fond of asking, why Broad Churchmen do not go out of the Church, you may give the simple but cogent reply, because of the Act of Parliament 28 & 29 Vict. c. 122, which was framed for the express purpose of keeping them in.

The Church of England.

II.

THE LAITY.

"So many as intend to be partakers of the holy communion shall signify their names to the curate at least some time the day before. And if any of these be an open and notorious evil liver, or have done any wrong to his neighbours by word or deed, so that the congregation be thereby offended, the curate, having knowledge thereof, shall call him and advertise him that in any wise he presume not to come to the Lord's table, until he hath openly declared himself to have truly repented and amended his former naughty life, that the congregation may thereby be satisfied which before were offended; and that he hath recompensed the parties to whom he hath done wrong, or at least declare himself to be in full purpose so to do as soon as he conveniently may." — Rubrics before the Communion Service.

The Church of God, we have seen, is—and in the nature of things must be—a broad Church; it must be in fact co-extensive with the race. Reflection teaches us that unless the Creator cared for all His creatures He would be unworthy of the name of God. It is impossible therefore that He should have made special provision for the salvation of a small fraction of mankind, and ruthlessly left all the rest to be damned. The only thing which offers the shadow of justification for such a horrible doctrine is the great diversity which exists in men's religious thoughts and observances. But diversity is perfectly compatible with unity. We have found this out in the sphere of physical science. We are beginning to find it out in the sphere of religion. All the phenomena of nature may be summed up in the one word—Evolution. Similarly every religious thought, every religious ceremony, is the expression of a single instinct

—love for goodness; and the vast variety of phenomena in the religious sphere may all be summed up in the word Righteousness.

This, which we learn by reflection, we may also learn, as I pointed out, from the Bible. The author of the Apocalypse, it is true, speaks of the Church whose members are written in heaven as the Church of the first-born—that is, of Christ. But St Peter most distinctly declares that "in every nation he who worketh righteousness is accepted." The two statements put together amount to this: Christ is but another name for righteousness, and so the Church of Christ is the Church of righteousness. It is an eternal and universal Church, which existed long before the Christian era, and would continue to exist even if all the Churches of Christendom were to collapse. The members of the Church of Christ are written in heaven, simply and solely because they have worked righteousness upon earth.

Of this eternal and universal Church, it is evident, as I said, that local and temporary Churches —such as those of England, of Scotland, of Rome —can be at the best but parts. Not one of these

Churches—witness their excommunications and prosecutions and persecutions for heresy, witness their mutual jealousies and recriminations—not one of them has ever completely realised the scriptural and divine ideal of the Church; not one of them has ever completely realised its own local and partial character; not one of them has ever completely realised that righteousness—and righteousness alone—is sufficient for membership in the general assembly of the first-born. When this lesson has been learned—and not till then—the Churches of the world will become the Churches of our Lord and of His Christ.

So far in regard to the Church generally. As concerning the Church of England in particular, I said there were certain reasons which led me to believe that it was in reality broader than it seemed, that it had in fact made considerable progress towards the realisation of the ideal. The first of these reasons I explained to you last Sunday. The subscription required from the clergy has been enormously relaxed,—has been made as simple and as broad as it was possible for any subscription to be. "Unfeigned assent and consent to all and everything contained in the Prayer-book" was demanded before 1865. But since that date clergymen are only required to say they "believe that the doctrine of the Church as contained in the Prayer-book is not contrary to the Word of God." And, as I told you, the word doctrine in the new form of subscription is used in the singular number instead of in the plural, expressly to make provision for diversity of opinion. A clergyman may henceforth disagree with many of the doctrines contained, or apparently contained, in the Prayer-book, provided he accepts the doctrine as a whole. That doctrine is, and must be, expressed by the one word Christ; and a synonym for Christ is righteousness. "He gave Himself for us," says St Paul, for one sole purpose, "that He might redeem us from all iniquity, and purify unto Himself a peculiar people, zealous for good works."

That is the present attitude of the Church of England towards the clergy. And what of the laity? Here, too, there has been very marked improvement during the last thirty or forty years. Of course from the laity generally subscription has never been required. But the English universities used to exact it from all their members,—lay as well as cleric. In 1581 subscription to the Articles was enjoined by the Earl of Leicester, as Chancellor of the University of Oxford, to be required of all undergraduates at their matriculation, and from all Bachelors of Arts. This was abolished in 1854. Up to 1865 all Masters of Arts at Oxford were required to give, just like the clergy, unfeigned assent and consent to all and everything contained in the Prayer-book. It is hardly necessary to point out that the effects of this were frequently most pernicious. Bentham, for example, who had to subscribe to the Articles at the early age of twelve, declared that it left a stain upon his conscience which was never afterwards effaced; and he dissuaded the late Marquis of Lansdowne from coming to Oxford, on the ground that it was "a nest of perjury." Cambridge has never been in this respect so strict as Oxford; but even at Cambridge subscription was formerly required from every graduate before he could be admitted to a fellowship in his college. Now all these creed tests—I had almost said crude tests, and the word would have done as well—have been abolished in both universities. The highest honours and emoluments are open to any one who has sufficient learning, and who conducts himself like a gentleman.

But the point to which I am most anxious to call your attention to-day is this. According to the rubric which I read as my text, no one can be excluded from the Communion except an open and notorious evil-liver, or—this second clause is explanatory—one "who has done any wrong to his neighbour by word or deed, so that the congregation be thereby offended:" not such wrong as the best of us sometimes inflict on our neighbours through thoughtlessness or carelessness, but wrong whereby the congregation is offended. This "notorious" wrong would show that we were utterly and permanently regardless of our neighbour's welfare and indifferent to his misery. Evidently then our Church looks upon righteousness—or rather the absence of flagrant unrighteousness—as the sole qualification necessary for communicants. The Communion has always been regarded in every Christian Church, and I think rightly, as the most sacred and the most valuable of all the services. Yet for participation in this privilege in the English Church, no profession of faith can be demanded, no declaration of orthodoxy, not even the vaguest and most indefinite subscription, but only the absence of such conduct as would show a complete and settled antagonism to righteousness. Attendance at the Communion is the sign and the seal of Church membership. On the part of the communicant, it is the sign that he is in harmony with the spirit and aims of the Church. On the part of the Church itself, it is the acknowledgment and ratification of this harmony. This ratification our Church never refuses except to the notorious evil-liver. Narrow-minded clergymen have sometimes kept away intending communicants upon other grounds; I remember my own vicar did so on one occasion. But in all such cases it is open to the aggrieved parishioner to take legal action, and if he does so, the clergyman will inevitably be condemned; for he has committed an offence—a very grave offence—against the law of the land. A man may not accept the creed which was adopted for him by his godfathers and godmothers; he may no longer agree with the profession of faith which he made at his confirmation; he may be a very sceptic of sceptics; but, unless he is a notorious evil-liver, he cannot be refused admission to our Communion Service. The Church of England thus—implicitly at any rate—recognises the paramount, and indeed the sole, importance of righteousness.

And further, our Church also recognises the practical nature of righteousness, on which I have so often insisted. The notorious evil-liver is not the heterodox man, but the man who has done wrong to his neighbour. The Church of England — implicitly at any rate — accepts the great truth, first taught to the world by Christ, but since almost forgotten, that the service of man is the service of God, that an injury done to a fellow creature is the greatest, and indeed the only, injury which we are capable of inflicting upon the Deity. Since, then, unrighteousness is resolved according to our Church into wrong done to one's neighbour; and since wrong done to one's neighbour is indirectly, as I have often explained to you, wrong done to oneself:[1] it follows that the religion of our Church, whatever we may think about its accidental details, is *in essence* a religion which all wise men must accept, which all good men must love.

People tell us the Churches are doomed. Well, I do not know. Certainly the old narrow ecclesiasticism is doomed. But I have great hopes for the future of the Church of England. In the Act of Parliament of which I spoke last Sunday, and in the rubric of which I have reminded you to-day, lies its strength. According to that Act, our Church requires nothing from the clergy but assent to its general doctrine,—which is Christ or righteousness. According to the rubric, our Church excludes from its membership only those who are guilty of flagrant unrighteousness. And a Church which thus recognises the supreme importance of conduct need never die. I admit that clergymen often preach, and that laymen often speak, as if the Act had never been passed, as

---

[1] See a sermon on "The Partial and the Perfect Self," in my 'Origin of Evil.' The individual is part of the organism of humanity, in which, if one member suffer, all the members suffer.

if the rubric did not exist. But their ignorance does not alter facts. I admit that there are some things in the Articles and in our services incompatible with the Act and with the rubric. But these could easily be modified or removed. I admit that it may be possible, instead of continually broadening the Church until it becomes in all respects consistent with the Act and with the rubric, to keep on narrowing it in spite of both, till it would be no better than some wretched sect. And if this is done, believe me, the days of our Church are numbered. In the dark ages, the clergy could do what they liked, and the laity would do what they were bid. But times have changed. Now with the progress of education, now when the results of science and literary research are brought within the reach of the masses, a Church has no chance of living unless it appeals to the common sense, to the reason, to the moral instincts of mankind. And just in proportion as it makes this appeal, will it be strong and flourish and grow. Righteousness is essential—of all things most essential—to the welfare of men. They can get on well enough without any particular creed, they can get on well enough without any special ritual. But without righteousness they perish! The Church, therefore, which insists most upon righteousness, and least upon other things, is the best Church. The Church which insists solely upon righteousness is the only Church that will not pass away.

The Athanasian Creed.

I.

IN what I am going to say to you this morning about the Athanasian Creed, I shall confine myself entirely to *facts*—facts which you can all, if you please, verify for yourselves.

1. The Creed was not written by Athanasius. This is now admitted by all scholars, even the most orthodox, for the following reasons. (*a*) There is no trace of such a creed in any of the older MSS. of the works of Athanasius. (β) Athanasius himself disclaims as superfluous the use of any creed except the Nicene. (γ) There is no evidence of the existence of such a creed before, at any rate, the end of the eighth century. Its authorship has been attributed to a great

number of different writers; but on this point nothing definite has been proved. The Creed is not an original composition, but a compilation of sentences, taken chiefly from the writings of St Augustine. How the name of Athanasius came to be attached to it I do not know. One of our highest ecclesiastical authorities, Dr Swainson, declares that it was "an intentional and deliberate attempt to deceive and to procure for the Creed more respect than it would otherwise have obtained." This may be so; for Athanasius always had a great reputation as an orthodox theologian—he has been called indeed the father of orthodoxy. But even if the Creed were produced under his name in the honest conviction that it really represented his views, the fact remains that he was not its author. This does not, however, necessarily detract from its value. For Athanasius himself lived after the time when, according to the orthodox view, inspiration had ceased, and he was therefore just as liable to error, just as far from being infallible, as any subsequent writer.

The strongest objection to the Creed, ecclesiastically speaking, is the fact that it has never been sanctioned by any Œcumenical Council. Indeed, of the four councils whose authority alone is recognised by the Church of England, the last two—those, viz., of Ephesus and Chalcedon—solemnly prohibited the composition of any other creed than the Nicene. In the minutes of the Council of Ephesus we find the following remarks. "The holy synod has determined that no person shall be allowed to bring forward or to write any other creed, besides that which was settled by the holy fathers who assembled in the city of Nicæa with the Holy Ghost. But those who shall dare to compose any other creed, or to exhibit and produce any such, if they are bishops or clergymen, they shall be deposed; but if they are of the laity, they shall be anathematised." The Council of Chalcedon repeated the same prohibition. It is difficult to see how the recitation of the Athanasian Creed can be reconciled with that submission which our Church professes to the authority of these great Œcumenical Councils.

Well, that is the first point. The Athanasian

Creed was not written by Athanasius; and its author, whoever he was, composed it in opposition to the highest ecclesiastical authority.

II. The Athanasian Creed was written in Latin. In that language it is much simpler than it appears to be in English. The word person is a translation of the Latin word *persona*. Now *persona* has three meanings. (*a*) It stands first for an actor's mask. The word is derived, as you see, from *per*, through, and *sonare*, to sound. In ancient times actors wore masks, and these masks were called *personæ*, because the actor's words sounded or were uttered through them. (β) The word *persona* means the character which any one assumes, or the part which he plays, either on or off the stage. The *personæ* of an actor are the characters in his *répertoire*. And just as the same actor assumes many characters upon the scenic stage, so we all have to play many parts in actual life. Every individual in existence has more than one *persona*. You, for example, are a member of a family; that is one *persona*, it is one character in which you appear, one part which you play: you are a member of a profession; that is another *persona:* you are a member of a community; that is another *persona:* you are a member of a club, of a political party, of a railway company; these are other *personæ.* Cicero somewhere says, "Ego sustineo tres personas"—I am sustaining three characters, I appear before you in a threefold attitude. Here you have a very simple and intelligible instance of "trinity in unity." (γ) The word *persona* stands for one who appears in different characters—*i.e.,* for an individual. The third meaning corresponds to that of our English word person.

Now these are the only significations of the word *persona.* And it is manifest that in the Athanasian Creed we cannot understand the word in the first sense. No one supposes that the "persons" of the Trinity are actual, material masks. Nor can we understand the word in the third sense. For if the "persons" of the Trinity were three distinct individuals we should have three Gods. We are therefore tied down to the second signification. The "persons" of the Trinity—according to the Athanasian Creed—are the different characters or manners or ways in which the Deity appears to us.

How far this view would have been acceptable to those of the fathers who wrote in Greek, I am not concerned now to inquire. They used the term ὑπόστασις to express the distinctions in the Trinity, and this is a word of much more varied and indefinite signification. At present I merely want to explain to you the original meaning of the Athanasian Creed. That Creed teaches, rightly or wrongly, that God reveals Himself in a threefold way—in nature, in Christ, and in our own hearts. The source of the three revelations —the divine Substance—is the same. "The Father is God, the Son is God, and the Holy Ghost is God, yet are they not three Gods but one God." In other words, it is the same kind and holy Being who appeals to us in the physical beauty of nature, in the moral beauty of Christ, and in those yearnings after moral perfectness which, do what we will, we can never completely extinguish.[1]

---

[1] See also a sermon on "The Triune God" in my 'Defects of Modern Christianity.'

Some who possess but a little knowledge of theology—which, like a little knowledge in any other department of study, is a dangerous thing—may perhaps say that this interpretation of the Athanasian Creed is Sabellian. Well, if it were, I could not help it. The fact would remain that no other interpretation was possible. But the view I have given you is not Sabellian. For Sabellius taught that the *personæ* of the Trinity were not coexistent but consecutive,—in plain English, that God revealed Himself first as the Father, afterwards as the Son, afterwards again as the Holy Ghost, and that the one revelation was over before the next began. But according to the Athanasian Creed, God is always revealing Himself in all three ways at once.

However, with the orthodoxy of the Athanasian Creed I am not now concerned. I simply want to tell you what that Creed actually says. And about this there can be no doubt; for the word *persona* has three and only three meanings, of which two are manifestly in the present case inadmissible. Adopting the only signification of the term which remains, we find the Athanasian

Creed declaring that God appears to us in three characters, that He reveals Himself to us in three ways, that He stands to us in a threefold relationship.

III. The damnatory clauses. What shall I say about them? Well, in passing, I should like to point out that, if they are to be believed, every one who accepts the English version of the Creed will most certainly be lost. For our word person means an individual; and three individuals in the Trinity would be equivalent to three Gods. Whoever, therefore, accepts the Athanasian Creed *in English* is a tritheist; he is guilty of having "divided the Substance"; and, if the damnatory clauses of the Creed be true, he will "without doubt perish everlastingly."

But they are not true. It is more impossible than that two straight lines should enclose a space. Belief in the Athanasian Creed necessary for salvation! Our eternal welfare depend upon our acceptance of some twenty sentences, which an unknown writer selected from St Augustine and others, and published under the false—not to say forged—name of Athanasius! No stranger, madder delusion ever took possession of a human mind.

And even if this Creed had been written by the "father of orthodoxy" himself, even if it had received the sanction of all the Œcumenical Councils, even if it expressed in the most satisfactory way the unanimous opinions of all Christian theologians, the fact would still remain that salvation by creed is not the salvation of Christ.

In a brilliant article which Professor Huxley contributed lately to the 'Nineteenth Century,' he finely said: "I verily believe that the great good which has been effected in the world by Christianity has been largely counteracted by the pestilent doctrine, that honest disbelief in creeds is a moral offence, indeed a sin of the deepest dye, deserving and involving the same future retribution as murder and robbery. If we could only see in one view the torrents of hypocrisy and cruelty, the lies, the slaughter, the violations of every obligation of humanity, which have flowed from this source along the course of the history of Christian nations, our worst imaginations of hell would pale before the vision." This "pestilent doctrine" as to the paramount importance of creed, I am bound to confess, has often been insisted upon by the Churches; but it is no part of the religion of Christ, nay, it is absolutely alien to the whole spirit and genius of His teaching.

No one since the world began ever laid less stress upon creeds than Jesus of Nazareth. The salvation which He preached was pre-eminently salvation by conduct. That is the one word which sums up the whole of His teaching—conduct, the conduct that springs from love. In His farewell address to the disciples, as recorded by St John, Christ Himself three times summarises His own teaching. "A new commandment I give unto you, That ye love one another. This is my commandment, That ye love one another. These things I command you, That ye love one another. By this shall all men know that ye are my disciples, if ye have love one to another." And St Matthew, who was as different a man intellectually from St John as it would be possible to find, nevertheless agrees with him in giving the same prominence to the fundamental thought of Christ. The Saviour asserted, St Matthew tells us, that our future destiny would depend upon our conduct here and now. "The King shall say unto them on his right hand, Come, ye blessed of my Father, inherit the kingdom prepared for you. For I was an hungered, and ye gave me meat: I was thirsty, and ye gave me drink: I was a stranger, and ye took me in: I was naked, and sick, and in prison, and ye ministered unto me. Inasmuch as ye did it unto one of the least of these my brethren, ye did it unto me."

Whoever, in the face of all this, maintains that we are to be saved by creed, gives the lie to Christ. I know of nothing sadder in the history of the world than the fact, that the "pestilent doctrine" has been so often preached by the Saviour's professed disciples. For the simple, practical, human, divine religion of Jesus, they have substituted a wretched system of definitions and formulæ and creeds. It has been, not unnaturally, supposed that the doctrines of those who called themselves disciples were really the doctrines of the Master Himself, that the doctrines of Christendom were always and necessarily the doctrines of Christ. No wonder, therefore, that Christianity has been attacked. Mr Cotter Morison, you remember, tells us that Christianity must be a demoralising religion, because it ignores conduct. If it did ignore conduct, it would be demoralising. But as I have explained to you before,[1] the Service of Man, which Mr Morison so eloquently preaches, is the very religion of Christ Himself; only instead of *substituting* the service of man for the service of God, as Mr Morison suggests, Christ identified the two. According to Christ, in learning to be kind we are working out our salvation; according to Christ, if we do our duty here it will be well with us hereafter; according to Christ, the service of man is the highest, and in fact the only, service which it is in our power to render unto God.

> "Abou Ben Adhem (may his tribe increase!)
> Awoke one night from a deep dream of peace,

---

[1] See 'Inspiration,' pp. 272-283.

And saw within the moonlight in his room,
Making it rich and like a lily in bloom,
An angel writing in a book of gold.
Exceeding peace had made Ben Adhem bold,
And to the presence in the room he said,
'What writest thou?' The vision raised its head,
And, with a look made of all sweet accord,
Answered—' The names of those who love the Lord
'And is mine one?' said Abou. 'Nay, not so,'
Replied the angel. Abou spoke more low,
But cheerly still, and said, 'I pray thee then
Write me as one that loves his fellow-men.'

The angel wrote and vanished. The next night
It came again with a great wakening light,
And showed the names whom love of God had blessed,
And lo! Ben Adhem's name led all the rest."

That was, that is, that eternally will be the religion of Christ. To substitute for this "the pestilent docrine" of salvation by creed, and to call *that* Christianity, is to be guilty of the greatest and cruellest crime which it is possible to commit; it is "to crucify the Son of God afresh and put Him to an open shame."

I hope that you agree with me. But, whether you agree with me or not, I tell you the time will come in the far-off future when all the world will acknowledge that what I said to-day was true.

The Athanasian Creed.

II.

LAST week I received a suggestive letter, part of which I will now read to you.

"The doctrine of the Trinity, as enunciated in the so-called Athanasian Creed, has hitherto been to my mind a mystery mystified; but your exposition of the *persona* feature opens up a meaning intelligible and reasonable, and which harmonises the Creed with the Apostles' and the Nicene.

"The damnatory clauses I have never repeated since I was old enough to comprehend words; but with the fuller apprehension of the meaning of the Creed which I now enjoy, I think them capable without any straining of such a construction, as will not only enable me for the future to give my assent to them, but may also induce you to withdraw your designation of them as a pestilent doctrine.

"Granting that a creed alone will not save any man—does any man *truly* hold a creed when his conduct is inconsistent with the doctrines therein set forth? . . . If a man says I admit a creed, but shows by and in his daily life that this is a mere assent of the lip, or even of the mind—his course of life giving, in fact, the lie to his professions—every one must admit that such a man is a mere hypocrite, and his pretended belief a mere sham.

"If this be so, if he only can be said truly to hold a creed whose conduct is influenced thereby, if the following of Christ's teaching be necessary to salvation, and if the doctrine of the Athanasian Creed be consistent with Christ's teaching, as I conceive it is,—surely the damnatory clauses are not pestilent?

"For me at all events they will have a new meaning; and when in the appointed services of the Church the Athanasian Creed comes to be read, I shall no longer hesitate to join in repeating them; as in so doing I shall not be hurling anathemas at any one, but merely insisting on the deep importance of entire self-surrender to Christ, and the absolute necessity of receiving and embracing His doctrine of love, if we would do our duty in this life and hope for happiness in the great hereafter."

I propose to-day and next Sunday to offer you some remarks suggested by this thoughtful letter.

First of all, with regard to the flood of light I threw upon the Athanasian Creed—it is quite true; I did. As it stands mistranslated in the English Prayer-book, it is meaningless. Three persons in one person is as much a contradiction in terms as a square circle or a circular square. But I explained that the Creed was written originally in Latin, and that *persona* means the character which a person assumes or the part which he plays. The teaching of the Athanasian Creed is, not that there are three individuals in the Godhead, but that the one indivisible God has revealed Himself to us in three characters, viz., as Father, as Son, and as Holy Ghost,—or, to put it more simply still, in nature, in Christ, and in the individual heart. This, as my correspondent truly says, is intelligible and reasonable. In fact it is the best account of the relation between God and man which has hitherto been formulated.

But as for the damnatory clauses, they practically consign to perdition an almost infinite majority of the human race. Only a few men, comparatively speaking, have ever heard of the Creed. And still fewer have attempted to assign to it any intelligible meaning. I do not suppose there was one person present in this chapel the other day, who was aware that the words were susceptible of an intelligible interpretation. Now I need hardly say that reciting words is not the same thing as believing propositions. Suppose, for example, I say to you in English that twice two make four, you will believe me. But if I offered you the same remark in Hebrew, you would not believe me, because until I translated it you would not know what I was talking about. Or suppose, again, I told you it was necessary for your everlasting salvation to believe in "abracadabra," and you accepted my assertion and determined to try. You might rise in your place every Sunday and recite the word—nay, after the manner of Stylites, you might stand on a pillar for thirty years incessantly shouting "Abracadabra, abracadabra, abracadabra!"—but inasmuch as it is a meaningless word, you would never have succeeded in believing in it; and if believing in it were essential to your salvation, you would, after all your pains, be damned. Repeating a number of sentences, without knowing the meaning of the words, is an exhibition of stupidity, not of faith. Declaring you believe that to which you can attach no meaning is not religion, it is one of the worst forms of immorality, it is lying. Only an infinitesimal number of nominal Christians—only those who understand what it means—are capable of believing the Athanasian Creed; and to say that those who do not believe it will without doubt perish everlastingly, is to say that they will be damned because there was no one to explain to them what it meant.

My correspondent however—who formerly refused to recite the damnatory clauses, but who now feels himself, owing to my sermon curiously enough, at liberty to do so in the future—says that he will not mean, when he repeats them, to hurl anathemas at any one, but merely to "insist on the deep importance of entire self-surrender to Christ, and the absolute necessity of receiving and embracing His doctrine of love, if we would do our duty in this life and hope for happiness in the great hereafter." Now it seems to me that the damnatory clauses are about as ill-suited to express this, as any collection of words which it would be possible to put together. Whosoever will be saved, they assert, must thus think of the Trinity. If we use the words in their ordinary sense, "thinking of the Trinity" and "embracing Christ's doctrine of love" are two totally different things. They may exist together, but they may just as easily exist apart. The one is a theoretical state of mind, the other is a state of heart and a mode of life. However, anybody has a right to use words in any sense he pleases, provided he tells us exactly the sense in which he does use them,—and keeps to it. If we understood the damnatory clauses in the way in which my correspondent interprets them, there would be less objection to our repeating them. But even in his sense they are not strictly true. He understands them to insist upon the deep importance of self-surrender to Christ, and the absolute necessity of receiving and embracing His doctrine of love, if we are to do our duty here and hope for happiness hereafter. Now those of you who are acquainted with the general scope of my teaching will be perfectly aware, that I have often and often insisted upon the deep importance of self-surrender to Christ,—such self-surrender that His spirit should become our spirit, such self-surrender that we should be able to say "Christ liveth in us." You will be aware that I have gone perhaps beyond any of my contemporaries in maintaining, that all morality and all religion were summed up in Christ's law of love, and that only when we received and embraced this law could we hope to make the best of our life here and hereafter. But you must remember that the great majority of the human race have never heard of Christ's law of love. To say, therefore, that those who have not received it will without doubt perish everlastingly, is to say that the immense majority of mankind will be eternally damned, and that through no fault of their own, but because Providence thought fit to place them in a position where the means of salvation were inaccessible. And it is self-evident that if the Supreme Power in the universe be just, in other words if there be a God, little will be required from those to whom little has been given; and therefore those who have never heard of Christ are in less danger of perishing everlastingly—if such a thing were possible—than some of us who fail to live up to our higher light.

My correspondent says that in repeating the damnatory clauses he will have no intention of hurling anathemas. As far as he is concerned, I accept his assurance without hesitation. But I cannot see that the mere fact of my having given an intelligible interpretation to the Athanasian Creed alters in any way the meaning of the damnatory clauses. They remain just as damnatory as ever. And you will observe that, by the very wording of them, they apply to others rather than to ourselves. They are throughout expressed in the third person,—not unless *I* think thus of the Trinity, *I* shall without doubt perish everlastingly, but *he;* unless he thinks thus of the Trinity, he will without doubt perish everlastingly. And I cannot help thinking that the constant recitation of the conditions under which other men are to be damned — even supposing those conditions to be correctly enunciated — I cannot help thinking that such a recitation is essentially demoralising. It is the old story of meddling with the mote in your neighbour's eye, when perhaps all the while a beam may be in your own eye. Those who recite, for example, the Athanasian Creed, always believe that they believe it, and that therefore they themselves will be saved. How infinitely more profitable it would be for them, if they were to recite instead the conditions under which they might be lost. Such, for example, as our Lord's words: "Not every one that saith unto me, Lord, Lord, shall enter into the kingdom of heaven; but he that doeth the will of my Father. Many shall say to me in that day, Lord, Lord, have we not prophesied in thy name? and in thy name cast out devils? and in thy name done many wonderful works? Then I will profess unto them, I never knew you: depart from me, ye that work iniquity." Or those words of St Paul: "Though I"—I, you will observe, not other people—"though I speak with the tongue of men and of angels, and have not love, I am become as sounding brass, and as a tinkling cymbal. And though I have the gift of prophecy, and understand all mysteries, and all knowledge; and though I have all faith, so that I could remove mountains, and have not love, I am nothing. And though I bestow all my goods to feed the poor, and though I give my body to be burned, and have not love, it profiteth me nothing." Or those words of the author of the Epistle to the Hebrews: "Leaving the principles of the doctrine of Christ, let us go on unto perfection. For it is impossible for those who were once enlightened, and who have tasted of the heavenly gift, and were made partakers of the Holy Ghost, . . . if they shall fall away, to renew them again unto repentance." The recitation of such passages as these would have a solemnising and stimulating effect upon the worshipper, and make him sensible of the necessity for care lest *he himself* should "become a castaway." Whereas the practice of calmly consigning others to perdition tends to foster a spirit of self-righteousness, quite incompatible with real religion, and still more incompatible with anything like religious progress. Nay, the practice may have such a hardening, damning effect upon the hearts of men and women, that at last they become absolutely incapable of comprehending Christ's law of love. I myself heard a clergyman say from the pulpit, "My brethren, you may imagine that when you look down from heaven and see your acquaintances and friends and relations in hell, your happiness will be somewhat marred. But no! you will then be so purified and perfected that, as you gaze on that sea of suffering, it will only increase your joy."

I should like you to contrast with that the following poem[1] of Walter Smith's:—

> "There came a soul to the gate of Heaven,
>   Gliding slow—
> A soul that was ransomed and forgiven,
>   And white as snow:
> And the angels all were silent.

---

[1] 'Hilda,' by the Rev. Walter C. Smith, published by James Maclehose & Sons, p. 102.

A mystic light beamed from the face
    Of the radiant maid :
But also there lay on its tender grace
    A mystic shade :
And the angels all were silent.

As sunlit clouds by a zephyr borne
    Seem not to stir,
So to the golden gates of morn
    They carried her :
And the angels all were silent.

'Now open the gate, and let her in,
    And fling it wide,
For she hath been cleaned from stain of sin,'
    St Peter cried :
And the angels all were silent.

'Though I am cleansed from stain of sin,'
    She answered low,
'I came not hither to enter in,
    Nor may I go : '
And the angels all were silent.

'I come,' she said, 'to the pearly door,
    To see the Throne
Where sits the Lamb on the Sapphire Floor,
    With God alone : '
And the angels all were silent.

'I come to hear the new song they sing
    To Him that died,
And note where the healing waters spring
    From His pierced side : '
And the angels all were silent.

'But I may not enter there,' she said,
    'For I must go
Across the gulf where the guilty dead
    Lie in their woe:'
And the angels all were silent.

'If I enter heaven I may not pass
    To where they be,
Though the wail of their bitter pain, alas!
    Tormenteth me:'
And the angels all were silent.

'If I enter heaven I may not speak
    My soul's desire
For them that are lying distraught and weak
    In flaming fire:'
And the angels all were silent.

'I had a brother, and also another
    Whom I loved well;
What if, in anguish, they curse each other
    In depths of hell?'
And the angels all were silent.

'How could I touch the golden harps,
    When all my praise
Would be so wrought with grief-full warps
    Of their sad days?'
And the angels all were silent.

'How love the loved who are sorrowing,
    And yet be glad?
How sing the songs ye are fain to sing,
    While I am sad?'
And the angels all were silent.

'O clear as glass is the golden street
    Of the city fair,
And the tree of life it maketh sweet
    The lightsome air :'
And the angels all were silent.

'And the white-robed saints with their crowns and
    palms
    Are good to see,
And O, so grand are the sounding psalms!
    But not for me :'
And the angels all were silent.

'I come where there is no night,' she said,
    'To go away,
And help, if I yet may help, the dead
    That have no day.'
And the angels all were silent.

St Peter he turned the keys about,
    And answered grim;
'Can you love the Lord, and abide without,
    Afar from Him?'
And the angels all were silent.

'Can you love the Lord who died for you,
    And leave the place
Where His glory is all disclosed to view,
    And tender grace?'
And the angels all were silent.

'They go not out who come in here;
    It were not meet:
Nothing they lack, for He is here,
    And bliss complete.'
And the angels all were silent.

'Should I be nearer Christ,' she said,
 'By pitying less
The sinful living, or woeful dead
 In their helplessness?'
And the angels all were silent.

'Should I be liker Christ were I
 To love no more
The loved, who in their anguish lie
 Outside the door?'
And the angels all were silent.

'Did He not hang on the cursed tree,
 And bear its shame,
And clasp to His heart, for love of me,
 My guilt and blame?'
And the angels all were silent.

'Should I be liker, nearer Him,
 Forgetting this,
Singing all day with the Seraphim,
 In selfish bliss?'
And the angels all were silent.

The Lord Himself stood by the gate,
 And heard her speak
Those tender words compassionate,
 Gentle and meek:
And the angels all were silent.

Now, pity is the touch of God
 In human hearts,
And from that way He ever trod
 He ne'er departs:
And the angels all were silent.

And He said, 'Now will I go with you,
    Dear child of love,
I am weary of all this glory, too,
    In heaven above :'
And the angels all were silent.

' We will go seek and save the lost,
    If they will hear,
They who are worst but need me most,
    And all are dear :'
And the angels all were silent."

Salvation by Creed.

THE doctrine of salvation by creed has been called, and I think justly, a pestilent doctrine. It involves one or other of two assumptions, both of which are false. It implies either that we are to be saved by creed without any reference to conduct; or that there is a necessary correspondence between the two, that if our creed be correct, our conduct will inevitably be right. The first assumption—that we are to be saved by creed without reference to conduct—has been much more common than you are perhaps aware. It is distinctly the teaching of high Calvinists; and it is in fact only a logical deduction from the doctrine of "justification by faith."[1] Did I

[1] Of course I know that this doctrine is often *professed* by those who recognise the importance of conduct. See note on Luther at the end of my 'Inspiration,' second edition.

ever tell you the story of the Scotch student who was being examined for orders, and was asked amongst other things what he thought of good works. Being anxious to show his orthodoxy, he replied, "Perhaps, all things considered, a man might not be much the worse for a few of them." That is not a parody,—it is a statement,—of the extreme view. Works have not only been regarded as of less value than faith, but they have been denied all value whatsoever; and indeed it has been maintained that a man had better be without them, than think that they had anything to do with salvation. It has been held that what would be a sin in an "unbeliever" is not a sin in the case of one of the elect. Whittier somewhere speaks—

> "Of Antinomians free from law,
> Whose very sins are holy."

This is one form of the doctrine of salvation by creed. It is not necessary for me, I hope, to say anything to show that it is a pestilent doctrine—the most pestilent with which ever the world was cursed.

The doctrine of salvation by creed, however,

has been more frequently held in another form. Those who proclaim it do not very often mean to ignore the importance of conduct, but only to emphasise the necessary connection which they imagine to exist between conduct and creed. They assume that the two will always vary directly, and that in so far as the creed is correct the conduct will inevitably be good. Now, no doubt this is a less objectionable form of doctrine, but it is nevertheless "pestilent," for it is false. There is no necessary connection between creed and conduct. As a matter of fact, they are constantly at variance. For example, you may believe that it is time to get up in the morning, and yet keep on lying in bed. You may believe that certain things disagree with you, and yet persist in eating them. You may believe that you have in you the makings of a great man, and yet, for want of taking the necessary trouble, remain after all nobody. My correspondent says that the man whose conduct does not agree with his creed is a hypocrite. But that is not the proper designation for him. The man is a hypocrite who says he believes what he knows he does not believe.

But your belief may be perfectly honest and sincere, although you do not act upon it. You may believe, with all the strength of conviction of which you are capable, in the righteousness of a certain course of conduct, and yet go and do exactly the opposite. Now this want of correspondence between your belief and your conduct is not hypocritical. On the contrary, you would only be guilty of hypocrisy if you attempted to justify your conduct by professing to believe that it was right.

If you reflect for a very little you will see that, so far from conduct always corresponding with creed, the same creed is often held by persons whose conduct is very different, and different creeds are often held by persons whose conduct is the same. Let me illustrate the last of these statements first. A friend of mine sat next to Cardinal Manning at a dinner-party one evening, and the night after found himself sitting beside Mr Frederick Harrison. Both these gentlemen talked to him about their work, about their sermons, about the sick people they had been visiting, about their philanthropic schemes, and so forth. My friend was struck with the similarity of their conversation, and he said to Mr Frederick Harrison—"Really I don't see much difference between you and Cardinal Manning." Mr Harrison smiled and said, " Upon my word I think you're right. My wife was saying to me only the other day that though she had always declared she wouldn't marry a clergyman, she was beginning to think she had married one after all,—that I was a regular parish priest." There could hardly be two more divergent creeds than Cardinal Manning's and Mr Harrison's; yet each of them is working hard and doing his best, spending and being spent, to ameliorate human lives. We may not approve of the methods of either of them. But that the conduct of both is in the main determined by the law of love, no one in his senses can for a moment doubt.

And not only may you have the same kind of conduct with different kinds of creeds, but you may also have different conduct with the same creed. The creed of the majority of Christians is practically the same, and yet what infinite diversity we find in their conduct. My correspondent would say, because some of them do not "truly" hold their creed. Ah! now we are coming to something. Let us see.

Evidently my correspondent admits—what all thoughtful persons must admit—that there is a true and false, a right and a wrong, way of holding a creed. In other words, *merely* holding it is not sufficient; the creed alone is not enough for salvation. I can best perhaps make you see what I mean by asking you to contrast the word creed with the word belief. The latter is more elastic in meaning than the former. The term belief may be applied to persons as well as to propositions. But not so the term creed. That means—and can only mean—the proposition or propositions to which mental assent is given. These propositions may be about persons, but all the same it is the propositions, and not the persons, which form the creed. Even in the verbal laxity of conversation you would never be said to have a creed in a person. But you may have a belief in him. This accounts for the fact that in the English version of the New Testament we find Christ, who never said anything about creeds, insisting upon the importance of belief, as in the well-known passage—

"God so loved the world, that He gave His only begotten Son, that whosoever believeth in Him might not perish, but have everlasting life." Now it is evident that believing in a person is something very different from mentally assenting to certain propositions regarding Him. And Christ Himself explained very definitely what He meant by belief. "Whoso eateth my flesh, and drinketh my blood, hath eternal life. Except ye eat the flesh of the Son of man, and drink His blood, ye have no life in you." This, as I have explained to you, is a vehement metaphor to express the absorption of His nature into our own. For such a union the word belief is not an adequate expression, or to say the least it is apt to be misleading. It suggests to us as a general rule rather an intellectual attitude of mind than a state of heart and a mode of feeling. However, when you do use the word belief in reference to Christ, you must remember that the only belief He recognised was a belief which involved feeling, emotion, enthusiasm, love, self-surrender, passion.

And even this Christ insisted on, not for its own sake, but as a means to an end. "If ye love me," He said, "ye will keep my commandments." He wanted men to love Him, because He knew that a strong personal attachment is the best stimulus to conduct. And conduct, according to Christ, was the one thing needful. Conduct alone, according to Christ, would determine a man's fitness for heaven or for hell. In His description of the last judgment He represents Himself as receiving men, not because they had "thought" in a particular way of the Trinity or of anything else, not even on account of their personal attachment to Himself, but because they had been kind. And he never suggested that, if their conduct were right, it would matter by what motive they had been impelled; or rather, perhaps I had better say, He constantly assumed that for right conduct, the motive was practically always the same. "Your father Abraham," He said, "rejoiced to see my day." In other words, all the good in all ages, whether they know it or not, *are* constrained by the love of Christ, *do* eat the flesh and drink the blood of the Son of man. Many of the best and noblest men now living are Agnostics,—what Dr Wace would call Infidels. The real Christ has been obscured by theology, and for the theological Christ they feel no admiration or sympathy. And yet, if Christ's account of the last judgment be correct, the same welcome in the future will be accorded to them, as to those who have been consciously following the Nazarene. They may say, "Lord, *when* saw we Thee an hungered, and fed Thee? or thirsty, and gave Thee drink? When saw we Thee a stranger, and took Thee in? or naked, and clothed Thee? Or when saw we Thee sick, or in prison, and came unto Thee?" But the reply will be, "Inasmuch as ye did it unto one of the least of these my brethren, ye did it unto me. Come, ye blessed of my Father."

Christ's salvation then—and indeed the only possible salvation—is salvation by conduct. If we would be saved, it is above all things necessary that we believe in the paramount importance of conduct. That creed, that one single article of faith, *is* necessary for salvation. For unless we believe this intellectually, we shall make no effort to do right. But I need scarcely tell you that those who proclaim the doctrine of salvation by creed are not thinking of any such simple faith as this. The creeds of Christendom have been for the most part very complicated matters, full of all sorts of metaphysical subtleties which could not have any conceivable effect upon conduct. For instance, all Christendom was kept for centuries in turmoil over the "filioque clause,"—as to whether the Holy Ghost proceeded from the Father, or from the Father *and the Son*. Now it is evident questions such as these can have nothing to do with conduct, and therefore can have nothing to do with salvation. And the simple belief in the paramount importance of conduct, though it be a necessary stepping-stone to salvation, will not of itself save us. So that even if this belief were intended, the doctrine of salvation by creed would still be pestilent, for it would still be false. "The law in our members," as St Paul puts it, "may war against the creed—against the law in our mind—and bring it into captivity to the law of sin which is in our members." We may see and approve the better course, and still persistently choose the worse. The best creed in the world will never save a single soul.

Christ's Plan of Salvation.

THE word salvation, as you know, is derived from *salus*, which means, primarily, health or wellbeing in general; and secondarily, only one particular form of wellbeing,—safety from external danger. These two meanings of the word salvation will serve to classify the religions of the world. They all come under one or other category. Many religions—all early and barbarous religions—mean by salvation merely safety,—safety from the anger of the deities. The rites and ceremonies of these religions are intended to propitiate divine wrath. The gods of savages, you know, are always in a chronic state of rage, which nothing but liberal bribes can allay. There is a spurious form of Christianity which comes under the same head. I daresay you have all, in your youth at any rate, heard the Christian scheme of salvation described pretty much as follows. The first pair of human beings did something which the Deity had forbidden. In His anger He determined to visit them—and the myriads upon myriads of their unborn descendants as well—with eternal torment. But the Son of the Deity interposed and offered Himself as a sacrifice. The torture of Christ appeased to some extent the divine indignation, and so far satisfied His requirements, that a certain number of the human race are to be saved, that is, rescued from hell.—In this scheme you will observe it is all a question of external danger. Nothing is said about the personal wellbeing of the saved, except in the sense of freedom from pain. There is not a word concerning character. Some of those who believed in this scheme have maintained that character was of no consequence at all, that the Deity let men off simply and solely in virtue of the compact between Himself and Christ. Others have asserted that the righteousness of the Saviour was "imputed" or transferred to believers, and that in this way it was possible for God to regard them as good, when all the while they were nothing of the kind.

This is the old-fashioned scheme of salvation in all its hideous nakedness. I know that something like it has been held for the last two thousand years by many noble men and women. But here we have another illustration of the fact that there is no necessary connection between creed and conduct: they were so infinitely superior to the God in whom they believed. It is true that this scheme has generally been dressed up and more or less disguised by other doctrines inconsistent with itself, such, for example, as the doctrine that God was just, or that God was merciful. It is manifest, of course, that the Being who authorised such a scheme of salvation would be in the highest degree cruel and unjust. And what a paltry salvation it is, even for the few to whom it is vouchsafed. It makes no provision for their real wellbeing. It is the sort of salvation which might come to a leper, rescued from the jaws of a lion or a tiger, but left, after all, to be eaten away by his disease.

The best religions have always aimed at saving men, not from pain, but from sin. And Christ's Christianity is especially remarkable in this respect. I say Christ's Christianity, for there are plenty of other Christianities in the world. But *Christ's* consists entirely in a scheme for perfecting the individual character. His salvation is neither more nor less than self-development. Christ's scheme was a very simple one. It is all summed up in a single word: He taught that men were to be saved by love. And if you look into the *rationale* of this, you will see that His plan of salvation is profoundly philosophical, perfectly in harmony with the best ethics and the highest metaphysics of to-day.

Paradoxical as it may sound, selfishness is the great obstacle to self-development. Each of us is an individual, and each of us is apt to forget that he is also something more. We are parts of an organism. The isolated individual, as Caird points out, is not properly speaking a man, but only a fragment of humanity, as really dead as an amputated limb, which, in being cut off from the organism, is virtually cut off from itself.

"Considered from a merely individualistic point of view, the duties which we owe to family, state and race, the taking upon ourselves the heavy weight of their many burdens—all this is a limit to our freedom. But considered from a higher point of view, it is just here that there is provided an escape from the narrowness and poverty of the individual life, and the possibility of a life which is other and larger than our own and yet is at the same time most truly ours. For to be ourselves we must be more than ourselves. What we call love is, in truth, the finding of our own life in the life of another, the losing of our individual self to gain a larger self. As the scope of our sympathy widens till it embraces the complex life of the family, the nation, the race, at each successive step we are only expanding the range of our own moral life, escaping further and further from the finitude of the individual self, and approximating more and more to a life which is unlimited and universal." And unless we enter upon this inheritance of the universal life, we shall never be truly perfect. A man cannot realise himself within himself, cannot come to perfection by himself, but only in and through communion with others. Well has Mr Phillips Brooks said, there are some parts of the individual's life which are always in his brethren's keeping, and which he can only receive from them. A deeper self-hood, a richer personality comes to a man from communion with others and sacrifice for others, than he could possibly have gained by any amount of solitary contemplation or self-aggrandisement. It is only as our individual, narrow, exclusive, isolated self is developed into a larger, inclusive, sympathetic self, that we come to our highest life. "To go forth out of self, to have all the hidden wealth of feeling of which I am capable called forth towards others, and to receive back again this wealth redoubled, in reciprocated affection and increased power of loving,—this is to live wisely and well; not to do this is to eliminate from life all that makes it most truly human, all that makes it most really valuable." Selfishness, therefore, is the great barrier to our highest self-development. To live for the isolated self is to die.

But if we are to merge our own life in that of

others, if we are to live for others as well as for ourselves, we shall, in the first instance at any rate, be called upon to suffer. The narrower self resents being developed; so the development can only be accomplished by conflict and pain. And since it is necessary to our self-development, the self-denial which Christ asks of us is a reasonable service. In this respect it is to be distinguished from asceticism.

A great many moralists and philosophers have insisted on self-surrender because they despised and depreciated the individual. Gautama, the founder of Buddhism, maintained that belief in one's own personality was an illusion which ought to be as speedily as possible dispelled: and he taught his disciples to look forward to extinction as the highest good. Buddhists, therefore, regard the mesmeric trance, in which all consciousness is lost, as the sublimest conquest of mind over matter—the nearest approach to perfection which is possible for us on this side annihilation. The philosophies of the Neo-Platonists and others are dominated by a similar notion. They teach that as God is one, human individuality (which of course involves plurality) must be something different from God, and therefore bad. Hence in these systems the highest form of mental activity is represented as a sort of swoon, in which the sense of personality is lost and the individual spirit is absorbed into the divine.

Christ did not insist on self-denial from any such notions as these. He did not inculcate it because He thought less of the individual than others, but because He thought more. The preciousness of *every* human being was one of our Lord's most fundamental doctrines. "How think ye?" He said to His disciples, "if a man have an hundred sheep, and one of them be gone astray, doth he not leave the ninety and nine, and goeth into the mountains, and seeketh that which is gone astray? And if so be that he find it, verily I say unto you, he rejoiceth more over that sheep, than over the ninety and nine which went not astray. Even so it is not the will of your Father which is in heaven, that one of these little ones should perish." His belief in the importance and infinite value of the individual may be traced throughout the whole of the Saviour's teaching.

In harmony with this is Christ's view of self-denial. One kind of moral training uses self-denial as a punishment or atonement. Because you have done so much which you ought not to have done, you shall surrender so much pleasure and suffer so much pain; or if you will endure a certain number of fastings and flagellations, you may be allowed a certain amount of indulgence in your favourite vices. Another use to which self-denial is sometimes applied, is to express the essential badness of the thing surrendered. Because the earth is inherently and altogether wicked, therefore by all means in your power endeavour to cultivate disgust for it. But with Jesus, self-sacrifice is always a necessary means to a reasonable end, and that end is self-development. We lose our life in order that we may truly gain it. This is what gives, it has been well said, to the self-denial which Christ demands of us, "a triumphant and enthusiastic air." Not because you have not deserved to enjoy it, not because it is wicked to enjoy it, but because there is another enjoyment, or it may be something better than enjoyment, more worthy of your nature, therefore let this inferior enjoyment go.

It is instructive to contrast the kingdom of Christ with the republic of Plato. In Plato's ideal State the individual was regarded as existing merely for the good of the community, and on behalf of the community he was entirely and ruthlessly sacrificed. All the details of his life—his prospects, his profession, his marriage, and so forth—were to be arranged for him by the State, just as the State thought best. The individual was to be allowed nothing, which would not be directly conducive to the welfare of the society of which he was a member. But in the kingdom of Christ, on the other hand, nothing is demanded from the individual which is incompatible with his own wellbeing. He is required to sacrifice himself for others,—but only in such ways as indirectly conduce at the same time to his own highest good, only to such an extent as is absolutely necessary for his own complete development.

This complete self-development Christ represented as the whole duty of man. Our present and everlasting salvation was to be effected, He taught, through love. It may appear at first sight strange, that in summarising His doctrine He said nothing about our duty to God. "A new commandment I give you, That ye love one another. This is my commandment, That ye love one another. These things I command you, That ye love one another." He does not, in this summary of His teaching, command us to love God. It was not necessary; for the love of God is involved in, or at any rate will follow from, the love of others. "He that loveth is born of God; he cannot sin, because he is born of God." Apart from human love, there can be no genuine love of God. "If a man loveth not his brother whom he hath seen, how can he love God whom he hath not seen?" "That is not first which is spiritual, but that which is natural, and afterward that which is spiritual." And long before we come to love God consciously as God, unselfishness will help us to serve Him. There is only one thing we can do for the Almighty, and that is to perfect ourselves and our race. Many so-called infidels and atheists are amongst the most zealous servants of God. They—

> "Adore and worship, when they know it not;
> Pious beyond the intention of their thought,
> Devout beyond the meaning of their will."

Do you not see, then, how reasonable and beautiful is the religion of Christ? It has no angry Deity requiring to be bribed. No sacrifice is demanded of the individual which does not carry with it its own exceeding great reward. All that is asked of us is that we perfect ourselves. There is no contradiction between this world and the next, between the claims of God and of man. To do our duty in the present life is to prepare for the future. The service of man is the service of God. The welfare of humanity is the glory of the Deity.

This is the only salvation worthy of the name. "There is none other name under heaven given amongst men whereby we can be saved but the name of Jesus Christ." His method is not only the best, but it is the only possible, method of complete salvation.

The Connection between Creed and Conduct.

I RECENTLY received the following letter:—
"May I ask you to explain your meaning in saying that creed has no connection with conduct? If that be so, is not the argument against a cruel or degraded creed weakened? Did the savage cruelty of the Jews towards their enemies bear no relation to their belief that God was the avenger of His people Israel, not the Father of mankind? Were not the horrors of the Inquisition the natural outcome of the medieval belief in a materialistic hell? And did not the gloomy tenets of the Scotch Covenanters bear fruit for good and ill in their stubborn resistance and their terrible sternness?

"Thank God, many people are better than their creeds; and no doubt there are many who have calmly accepted the cruellest doctrines without question, and who would deem doubt devil-born, whose hearts have been nevertheless full of tenderest pity and kindliness. But in most of such instances can the believers be said to give even an intellectual assent to their creeds? Is it not rather a state of passive acquiescence in what they have been taught?

"On the other hand, there are doubtless many who hold that God is Love, and whose lives fall lamentably short of any realisation of that belief. But surely he whose creed teaches him to regard the object of his worship as a Being capable of acts of capricious cruelty such as we should shrink from with horror in a man,—a Being who could condemn His creatures to everlasting torment for not assenting to certain doctrines, would be more likely, if he really believed his creed, to be cruel and revengeful himself, than one who would formulate his religious belief in the words, 'What doth the Lord require of thee, but to do justly and to love mercy, and to walk humbly with thy God?'

"That also might be defined, might it not? as

in itself a mere statement to which we could give an intellectual assent, without our conduct being in the least affected. But if we passed beyond the stage of intellectual assent to that of faith, would not conduct follow? And if from giving an intellectual assent to the damnatory clauses we passed to the stage of faith in a God who could so act, would not our whole tone of thought about Him, and consequently our conduct, be lowered?"

Now I am always grateful for letters of this description. Sometimes they may show me that I have made a mistake; sometimes they may arise from a misapprehension on the part of the writer; but in all cases they are useful. What one person takes the trouble to write, probably a hundred persons think; and it is only a letter which would call forth from me the further explanation that is needed.

In the present case the writer is mistaken as to what I really said, unless through a slip of the tongue I said what I did not mean. I said—at any rate I meant, which is the important thing—not that there was no connection between creed and conduct, but that there was no *necessary* connection. There is all the difference in the world between these two statements. I should like in passing to ask you always to pay special attention to adjectives and adverbs. They are quite the most important parts of speech. I remember once in my ladies' class laying down the statement that character was determined mainly by circumstances. After the lecture I received a number of letters protesting against my doctrine—the writers called it *my* doctrine—that character was determined entirely by circumstances. To which my reply was a very simple one—viz., that it was not my doctrine. If I had held that character was determined *entirely* by circumstances, I should not have said *mainly*. So in the present case. From the illustrations used in the letter, it is evident the writer agrees with me that though there is, or may be, a connection between creed and conduct, the connection is not necessary, not constant, not invariable.

Let us ask why not? It will help us, I think, to arrive at a clear understanding of the matter if we notice the various ambiguities attaching to the word creed. It is used in different senses; it is applied to mental and moral conditions which are totally dissimilar.

(*A*) A creed may mean what a man professes to believe but does not. Let me refer again, by way of illustration, to the English version of the Athanasian Creed. That would commonly be said to be the creed of all those who stand up in church and recite it, though there is not one in ten thousand of them who attaches to it any intelligible meaning. Unless it has been explained in the way I explained it, it cannot possibly be believed. For as I pointed out to you, any one who understood the word "person" in the English sense of an individual, would be guilty of "dividing the Substance," and would therefore, according to the Creed, without doubt perish everlastingly. To avoid this fate he must understand the word in some other sense. But the ordinary man—"the plain man," as he is called by philosophers—does not know of any other signification. He does not know that the Creed was written in Latin, and that *persona* has several meanings. In saying the Creed he must not attach to the word person the only meaning with which he is acquainted. On pain of perishing everlastingly, he is obliged therefore to attach to the term no meaning at all. But the meaningless cannot be believed. It is impossible to believe in mere sounds. No propositions can be believed except those which have a definite and intelligible signification.

Of course it is open to any man to *profess* anything. Suppose I offer a small boy five shillings if he will say he believes that "abracadabra" is "camaraloupton"; he may try very hard, but though he may succeed in acquiring the money, he will not succeed in acquiring the belief. I do not say that all those who declare their belief in unintelligible propositions are absolutely dishonest. Because they can attach a meaning to the words taken separately, they may very likely imagine they understand them taken together. They may believe they believe. But that is all. And thinking one can accomplish the impossible is not the same thing as actually accomplishing it.

Now manifestly a creed which is merely professed—a creed which is not believed—cannot influence conduct. Between creed *in this sense* and conduct, not only *is* there no connection, but there *can be* none. You cannot act in accordance with the incomprehensible. What is absolutely meaningless cannot be a motive to action.

(*B*) The word creed may be restricted to that which is actually believed. But even in this case there is a still further ambiguity to be noticed. The term may be applied (1) to what we believe and merely believe, and (2) to what we believe and also love. A man may, and sometimes does, love that in which he believes. Hence it seems to be supposed that love forms part of every creed, or at any rate goes along with it, or to say the least, would go along with it if the creed were honestly and sincerely accepted. Now I want you to see this is not the case. A man may accept a creed without caring about it, without taking any interest in it, without feeling any enthusiasm for it: and in this case it will not and cannot influence his conduct.

To accept a creed, strictly speaking, is merely to assent to certain propositions. It is a purely intellectual condition. Whoever understands the meaning of the words, and thinks that they express what is true, has accepted the creed in question. There are many people in England to-day, there are probably some of them among us this morning, who believe the Apostles' Creed—really and thoroughly believe it, although its doctrines have never aroused in their hearts the faintest sentiment or emotion. They are quite certain that its statements are true; they have no doubt as to the facts; they feel quite sure that Christ "was born of the Virgin Mary, suffered under Pontius Pilate, was crucified, dead and buried, descended into hell, rose again the third day from the dead, ascended into heaven," and so on. Yet they do not care for Christ. He is nothing to them. They have less admiration for Jesus than they have for—say Napoleon or Bismarck. Christ is a less interesting personality to them than some of their neighbours and acquaintances. But mark you, they are not dishonest; they are not insincere. They are simply callous. You cannot say they do not believe *sufficiently*. So far as belief goes, there may be no difference between them and the most enthusiastic followers of the Nazarene. What is wrong with them is, not that they do *not* believe, but that they *merely* believe. Belief is the beginning and the end of what they blasphemously call their religion.

You can now see the reason, can you not? why men's creeds may be precisely identical, and yet their conduct totally different. Belief is no motive. Unless a man cares for what he believes, unless it excites in him interest, love, enthusiasm, he might, so far as his conduct is concerned, just as well be without it. It is not what we believe that determines our actions, but what we love. The connection between creed and conduct—even when it exists—is always indirect. If our creed does not supply us with something to love, if we do not care for the persons or things of which it treats, it will have no effect upon our actions. And even when we do find in it something that calls forth our affection and enthusiasm, it is these—the affection and enthusiasm—which determine our conduct, and not the creed itself. For that may exist in other men's minds, without producing any effect upon their hearts; and in such cases there will be no correspondence between what they believe and what they do. "With the heart man believeth unto righteousness;" with the heart man believeth unto every form of conduct. In other words, conduct only follows from creed through the intervention of love.

Now it is ridiculous to call that which a man supremely loves by a name which implies no affection whatsoever. All motives involve emotion. And to express the strongest emotion of all, the word creed is not only misleading, it is the worst possible word we could find. The best term would be perhaps ideal.

Unless a man's creed is a very simple one, it will never be more than partially embodied in his ideal. There is much in the creeds of Christendom, for example, which—whether true or not—could never excite any affection or enthusiasm. Such parts of the creeds will always, either consciously or unconsciously, be left out of our ideals, and will never therefore have any effect upon our conduct. Just consider what an infinite difference there is—so far as possible effect upon conduct is concerned—between the two statements, "I believe in the Holy Ghost," and "I believe that the Holy Ghost proceeds from the Father and the Son." To believe in the Holy Ghost is to believe that the Infinite Spirit may, and does, enter into communion with our spirits. Here is a thought which may well excite our enthusiasm and call forth our love. And if it does, we shall be stimulated to walk worthy of this high vocation wherewith we have been called, to conduct ourselves as becometh the children, the sons, the friends of God. But to believe that the Holy Ghost proceeds from the Father and the Son—even supposing it can be done, even supposing it is possible to attach any definite meaning to the words—is at best but to accept a proposition in technical theology. In the Greek Church men are taught to believe that the Holy Ghost proceeds only from the Father. Yet no one can suppose that their conduct is, on this account, worse than that of Roman Catholics or of English Churchmen. No one can suppose that the conduct of a single member of the Greek Church would be in one iota altered, by his coming to believe that the Holy Ghost proceeded from the Father *and the Son.*

I shall continue this subject, if all be well, another day, and point out to you more fully how ideals are connected with creed on the one hand and with conduct on the other. But I have already, I hope, said enough to convince you once and for ever that the important thing is not what you profess to believe, nor even what you actually do believe: your destiny here and hereafter will depend upon your conduct; and that will be determined by what you love. You may believe much, and have a low ideal. You may believe little, and your ideal may be transcendently sublime. Many good persons feel sad and anxious at the breaking up of the old orthodoxy, at the increasing disinclination on the part of the highly educated to accept the old ecclesiastical formularies. But for their comfort I would suggest that if, along with all this heresy, there exists, as I think there does, an ever-growing sense of the paramount importance of conduct, the world is after all progressing,—progressing, perhaps, by means of those very changes which they so deeply deplore. Like Elijah of old they say—"We, only we, are followers of the

Lord." But they are mistaken. God fulfils Himself in many ways,—ways undreamed of in their philosophy. "What they know not now, they will know hereafter." And I am sure I do them no more than justice when I say, they will be unfeignedly thankful when they find that they were wrong.

Ideals.

THERE is no necessary connection, we have seen, between creed and conduct. A man's creed may be good and his conduct bad. He may have no creed at all—at least nothing that would ordinarily be called a creed—and yet his conduct may be sublime. People who hold the same creed—who really believe in the accuracy and truth of its statements—nevertheless often act in different ways; and people who hold different creeds often act in the same way. The fact is, as I said, men's actions are determined, not by what they believe, but by what they love. Everything we care for has some effect upon our conduct. What we care for supremely determines the quality of our conduct upon the whole, —makes it in the main either good or bad. And that which a man cares for supremely may be called, as I suggested, his ideal.

Now, ultimately, there are only two kinds of ideals. They may all be classified under two categories. They are all concerned either with pleasure or with character, either with self-aggrandisement or with self-development, either with getting good things or with becoming good. We see every day around us proofs of the fact that men act in accordance with one or other of these ideals. Some will not hesitate to enrich themselves by what is called sharp practice; others would rather be beggared than do anything in the least degree ignoble. Some endeavour chiefly and generally to procure enjoyment for *themselves;* others are more anxious to give it to *their neighbours.* Some, as they grow older, become wiser, nobler, greater; others show no signs of development from their manhood to their grave. It is frequently quite manifest to which of these classes a man really belongs. But, manifest or not, every one does belong to one or to the other. He may scarcely know it himself; but if he sits down in a quiet moment to "cast up life's chequered sum," he will find that upon the whole he has given the preference either to pleasure or to character, he has thought most of what he could get, or most of what he might become, he has had one or other of the two ideals—self-aggrandisement or self-development.

I said last week that it was not the whole of a man's creed which affected his conduct, but only such parts of it as he really cared about, only such parts as were capable of exciting his emotion and enthusiasm. Now the portion of his creed which will interest him will depend upon his ideal. Let us look into this matter somewhat fully.

Theological creeds—and with these we are here chiefly concerned—all, or nearly all, speak both of happiness and righteousness. No doubt, unless the universe be fundamentally irrational, these two things must be *finally* coincident. Unless the universe be fundamentally irrational, the highest and most enduring happiness must be unattainable apart from righteousness; and on the other hand, righteousness must eventually lead to the supremest joy. But the moral difference between men consists in the degree of importance which they attach to each. One man thinks much of happiness and little of righteousness. Another is eagerly anxious for righteousness, and comparatively indifferent to happiness. When the two for a time clash the one man will sacrifice happiness without any hesitation, while the other will be equally ready to sacrifice righteousness. And a man's ideal for the next world will always correspond to his ideal for this. He will want there what he wants here. Hence it happens that the selfsame creed will present different aspects to different individuals. Two persons may believe it all, yet each may attend only to a part of it; and in this case it will *practically* have for them two totally different meanings. It is a psychological law that our power of attention is limited. When we attend earnestly to any particular thing, other things connected with it are more or less ignored and in time entirely forgotten. So far as mere words go, the creeds of the great Churches of Christendom are pretty much the same, and they are all based professedly on the language of the Bible; yet there are two diametrically opposite doctrines as to the nature of Christ's plan of salvation. According to some it is a mere scheme for keeping men out of hell. According to others it is a method for making men noble, Christlike, divine. The man with the low ideal is perfectly satisfied with the first result; or, at any rate, he is not concerned at all with the second. The orthodox heaven is certainly not a very attractive place, and he would much rather remain here. But, to say the least, it is the less of two evils; and any scheme therefore for enabling him to attain it naturally calls forth his interest. The man with a high ideal, on the contrary, knows that he might escape what is popularly called hell, or any other place of torment, — and still be lost; for the only salvation which he cares about supremely is a salvation from sin, a salvation of character.

It is a man's ideal, you see, which determines the part of his creed which he attends to—the part of his creed which he acts upon. One man will be attentive when the creed speaks, or seems to speak, of the way to avoid pain. And like all those who are very eager for pleasure, he is apt to miss it by being in too much of a hurry. He does not stop to inquire for the real meaning of his creed. He seizes upon any superficial meaning that first occurs to him. So when his creed tells him, or seems to tell him, that if he believes certain things he will not go to hell, he sets to work and tries. He would believe anything, just as he would do anything, for gain. When his creed tells him, or seems to tell him, that he must give up certain pleasures in order to secure greater pleasures by-and-by, he sets to work again and does it. What he calls his religion is a mere speculation,—a business transaction between himself and God. Another man, as he reads the selfsame creed, thinks little, if at all, of what it says about happiness, but pays the greatest attention to what it says regarding conduct. Anything in it which seems to suggest to him how he may become a higher type of man, anything in it which seems to point out a method for self-improvement and self-development,—these things at once excite his interest and call forth his enthusiasm. And so when the creed speaks of believing in Christ, of loving Christ, of following Christ, he endeavours to act up to it,—not for the sake of the happiness which is to follow, but for the sake of the goodness.

It is in this way, then, that a man's creed affects, or may affect, his conduct, not directly, but indirectly, through his ideal. It affects his conduct when it shows him, or seems to show him, how he may best attain to that which he supremely loves.

To some extent the ideal may be modified by the creed. No creed will change it altogether. Belief alone will never make a man prefer goodness to pleasure, any more than it would make him prefer music to mathematics. Likes and dislikes are not determined by the mind. No doubt many a man who loves pleasure supremely, has a lurking belief that he is living an ignoble life. But the belief is a mere belief. It never calls forth any sentiment or emotion strong enough to prompt him to corresponding conduct. And so a man who loves goodness supremely, even though he may believe that it will never have a reward, even though he may believe that the wages of virtue are dust, will still do what is right "in the scorn of consequence." Every man loves supremely either enjoyment or goodness; and no mere belief will lead him to transfer his affection. His creed will not make him love pleasure, nor will it make him love goodness. But it may raise or lower his standard in either case. He may discover in his creed suggestions as to the kind of pleasure which awaits him in the future, or as to the nature of the goodness which should be regarded as highest and most divine. Some men have found in so-called Christian creeds the assurance that the most Satanic kind of enjoyment would be the final endowment of the saved. One "father" of the Church has declared that the chief pleasure of heaven would consist in the contemplation of the lost in hell. And even the lovers of righteousness have been led, by some of the same creeds, to form a very low conception of the character of God. Let us take by way of illustration the two cases mentioned in the letter I read you last week—viz., the Scotch Covenanters and the Spanish Inquisitors. By a little careful analysis we shall see, I think, that the creed may often modify the ideal, and in so doing it will have a proportionate effect upon conduct.

In the history of the world perhaps there have been none who loved goodness more unselfishly, none who had a greater contempt for pleasure bought at the cost of right, none who more consistently, enthusiastically, unflaggingly obeyed the dictates of their conscience, than the old Scottish Covenanters. And yet they were not lovable. They were cold, hard, stern, unforgiving, intolerant. How was this? Why, it was, as my correspondent truly said, owing to their creed. All these unamiable qualities they believed to belong to Him, whom they at the same time held to be supremely good. He was going to consign the great majority of the race to eternal torments. He would never forgive sin—not even inherited sin—except in the case of the elect. And the very elect were required to give Him the whole of their thoughts and affections, in violation if necessary of every natural instinct. It seems strange that they should have regarded such a Being as good. But they did.[1] If they would be like their God therefore—and this was their supreme desire, because they believed Him to be infinitely good—they, too, must possess the same repellent characteristics.

So also with the Spanish Inquisitors. The most reliable historians are agreed that many, if not the majority, of them were actuated by the purest motives and the strictest sense of duty. Their creed taught them that God—the infinitely good Being—would not, could not, save a heretic; that all outside the pale of the Church were inevitably doomed to eternal flames. And so they were led to martyr the individual out of their very love for the race. They felt that sooner or later men would be frightened into orthodoxy and terrified into heaven.

In these and similar cases, you see, the connection has been very close and definite between creed and conduct. But as I have said over and

---

[1] They sometimes attempted to reconcile His contradictory attributes by saying, that what was apparently hateful and cruel in His conduct was prompted by infinite purity, by infinite justice, by infinite hatred for sin.

over again, it is not a necessary connection. For other men have held the Covenanters' creed and not been Covenanters. Other men have held the Inquisitors' creed and not been Inquisitors. They have really believed the same doctrines, which made the Covenanters so unamiable and the Inquisitors so cruel. But though they have believed them, they have not attended to them; and so their ideal, whatever it is, has been unaffected thereby. Some men instinctively shrink from such doctrines. They may believe them, and yet they cannot bear to dwell on them. They feel, almost unconsciously, that they are wrong. They do not try to reconcile them with their own standard of goodness. When they think about these doctrines at all, they say to themselves, God may have reasons for His actions which they cannot understand. But *for them* goodness means kindness, gentleness, mercy. That is their ideal; an ideal which no creed about the Deity—however firmly they may believe it—is able in the least degree to alter.

As time goes on men learn to pay more respect to the teaching of their own moral instincts, and less to the verbal authority of creeds. So far from allowing their ideal to be modified by their creed, it is the creed which they try to bring into harmony with their ideal. All creeds notwithstanding, they refuse to believe in the wickedness of God!

Use and Abuse of Creeds.

I HAVE shown you that there is no necessary connection between creed and conduct, and sometimes no connection at all. I have explained to you that a man's conduct will be affected only by so much of his creed as he cares about, only by such parts of it as excite his interest and enthusiasm. In all but the very simplest and shortest creeds, there will therefore be much which can have no connection with conduct, because it has no connection with the emotions. It does not follow, however, that all the rest of the creed is worthless. Knowledge is valuable for its own sake. And a creed is just a short summary of knowledge, or of what is regarded as such. These summaries may be very useful, though they are also capable of being made very pernicious. Let us see.

Creeds are needed in every sphere of investigation. G. H. Lewes tells us, *e.g.*, in his 'Seaside Studies,' that for years very little progress was made in zoology, because the workers in that department of science had no definite creed to guide them. There is no antagonism between philosophy and creeds; on the contrary, creeds are the handmaids of philosophy. A creed means, etymologically and really, that which is believed. It is a register of results in the search for truth. It is a landmark showing the point which has been reached in the march of human thought—a march which can never have an end. A creed consists of the opinions arrived at in a certain age, by certain men, on certain subjects, which they have transmitted, or ought to have transmitted, for the guidance, and not for the extinction, of future thought and investigation. It is a starting-point, not a goal. Just as an invading army makes good each position gained by planting a citadel, in order that they may be better able to set forth again to larger and more certain conquests; so it is necessary that creeds should be constructed, in order that men may be better prepared for making further progress into the still outstanding, still unexplored realms of truth.

But there is always a danger that creed will crystallise into dogma, and then it becomes an unmitigated curse. The difference between the two things is this. A creed means that which is at present believed: a dogma means that which may never be disbelieved. There have been instances of this crystallisation of creed into dogma even in the history of philosophy. Look at Aristotelianism during the middle ages—when the logic and the physics and the metaphysics of Aristotle had been exalted into dogmas. The gospel of that period was the anagram which had been made out of the name of the Stagirite —"Aristoteles, iste sol erat." Human ambition rose no higher than to shine with a light borrowed from this "sol." Hardly any one dreamed of thinking for himself. The circle of human knowledge was made to coincide with the discoveries of Aristotle. There is a story told of a certain monk who had detected some spots on the sun, and who rushed to his father superior to tell him of the phenomenon. The reply of his "superior" must, I should fancy, have made a cynic of the monk for the rest of his life. "My son," said the holy and silly father, "I have read through Aristotle many times, and I find no mention of any such thing; therefore rest assured either your glass or your vision is defective." Another of these reverend fathers refused to look through a telescope, for fear he should see something which had never been observed by Aristotle. A certain professor of philosophy in Padua came to Galileo, and requested that he would explain to him the meaning of the word parallax, which he said he wished to refute, having heard that it was opposed to Aristotle's doctrine touching the relative situation of the earth. As late as 1624 the Parliament of Paris issued a decree, banishing all who publicly maintained theses against Aristotle. In 1629 it was decreed that to contradict the principles of Aristotle was to contradict the Church—and we know what that meant in those days. When Ramus solicited the permission of Beza to teach in Geneva, he was told "the Genevese have decreed, once for all, that neither in logic nor in any other branch of knowledge will they depart from the principles of Aristotle." In fact the Stagirite, poor man, through no fault of his own but through the folly of his disciples in converting him into a dogma, was very nearly becoming the father of a universal reign of ignorance.

Look again at Positivism, or rather Comtism. What brilliant originality and intellectual stimulus there was in Comte's earlier writings! But the later development of his system became a laughing-stock to his enemies and a mournful sorrow to his friends. Why? Just because the later development was dogmatic. It was to be decided by the priests of Positivism what theories the common people were to believe, and what subjects the men of science were to investigate. The High Priest of Humanity proposed to saddle the world, to quote Professor Huxley's expression, with a sort of Roman Catholicism *minus* Christianity.

Curiously enough the crystallisation of creed into dogma has been most common in theology, where there was least excuse for it. Mr Garbett in his Bampton Lectures defines dogma as "that on which has been set the seal of divine infallibility." But even admitting to the fullest degree the plenary inspiration of the Scriptures, creeds are not the Bible. They were made long after inspiration, in the orthodox sense, had ceased. Creeds therefore cannot have been inspired, and have no claim to be regarded as infallible. The absurdity of regarding them as infallible should be evident to any one who has read ecclesiastical history. If there were *one* dogmatic system, the whole of which the believers in dogma had always embraced, and none of which they had ever disputed, we could understand its being considered infallible. It would have in its favour, if not the *consensus gentium*, yet the *consensus ecclesiæ*. But there is no such system. Dogma, which is supposed to be indisputably certain, has always been the battle-ground of the fiercest and most protracted disputes. Even the Popes, from the very chair of St Peter, have given forth contradictory utterances. The truth is one and the same, but there are endless differences in the interpretation of it. The Bible is "the book where each his dogma seeks and each his dogma finds." These diversified and often contradictory interpretations cannot possibly express the mind of God, in the same way and with the same authority as the one unchanging truth which they are supposed to interpret. We have Homoousianism and Homoiousianism; Arianism and Athanasianism; the expiatory and revelatory theories of the Atonement; the Romish, Lutheran, and Zwinglian view of the Eucharist; eternal punishment, annihilation, universalism, and a hundred other incompatible doctrines,—all professing to be the correct interpretation of Bible truth. This contradiction amongst the dogmatists, I say, is sufficient to show the absurdity of dogma. Each man thinks his own system infallible; but every other man has just as much right to make the same claim for a totally different set of formulæ. And the dogmatists are not only ridiculous, but unconsciously they blaspheme. They assume that they have fathomed the Infinite, that they have a complete knowledge of God. There are few men in the present day who would suppose that the last word had been said, even yet, on geology or astronomy. But it is constantly assumed that in the third or fourth century men knew all that ever could be known about the Deity, and expressed their knowledge in words which can never be altered except for the worse.

The truly humble man, the really religious man, will not rest contented with the formulæ of the past. I dare say you have often heard from the pulpit lamentations that there is so little belief in the world. For myself I feel more inclined to lament over the fact that there is so little doubt. In theology we should all have the philosopher's spirit. "Philosophy," said Aristotle, is "the art of doubting well." Dogma may be defined as the art of believing ill. Dogma believes, or tries to believe, it knows all the truth, in order that it may thereby avoid the trouble of seeking any. Philosophy doubts whether it knows any, in order that it may seek all. To philosophise, or to doubt well, is to doubt, not as the Pyrrhonist, but as the Cartesian. Descartes says in his tract on Method, "As I made it my business in each matter to reflect particularly upon what might fairly be doubted and prove a source of error, I gradually rooted out from my mind all the errors which had hitherto crept into it. Not that in this I imitated the sceptics, who doubt only that they may doubt, and seek nothing beyond uncertainty itself; for, on the contrary, my design was simply to find ground of assurance, and cast aside the loose earth and sand, that I might reach the rock or the clay beneath."[1] Philosophy perceives that truth is high as heaven, deep as hell, broad as the universe, infinite as God, everlasting as eternity. Philosophy is painfully conscious that there is

> "A deep below the deep,
> A height beyond the height;
> Our hearing is not hearing,
> And our seeing is not sight."

What would you think of an athlete who was going to run a race, and who became so enamoured of the arrangements at the first end of the course, that while others were pressing on towards the goal, he contented himself with going round and round the starting-post? No less absurd is the man who imagines, as soon as he can repeat his

[1] It is in the same Cartesian spirit that Helen, in 'John Ward, Preacher,' says, "I would not *sign* a creed, even if it had been written by myself."

creed like a parrot, he has mastered truth. Truth cannot be symbolised by a circle, but rather by an infinite line. The men who think they have given the ultimate explanation of universal mystery, or of any part of it, must be fools. In the nature of things a finite mind can never do more than approximate to a knowledge of the infinite. But, generation after generation, we ought to be getting nearer to that full and adequate knowledge, which can never be actually attained.

> "Our little systems have their day,
>   They have their day, and cease to be;
>   They are but broken lights of Thee,
>   And Thou, O Lord, *art more* than they."

Reverence.

I.

ITS DEFINITION.

I DO not know anything more difficult than to give a satisfactory definition. And it is especially difficult to define a word which is constantly in everybody's mouth, but which is as constantly used in different senses. We have not only to say in what sense the word ought to be used, but also to explain how the illegitimate significations have come to be in vogue. Nor is this a mere question of words, a mere matter of terminology, that might be left to the dictionary makers. Not at all. The words which we use, especially in reference to morality and religion, and the way in which we use them,—all this is of the greatest possible moment; for the words are expressive of our ideas, and our ideas to a great extent determine our conduct.[1] There is perhaps nothing that will have a greater influence upon our welfare than the meaning which we attach to the word reverence. And yet the distinction between true and false reverence, between right and wrong reverence, has seldom, if ever, been drawn. We find acute and eminent writers who constantly mistake true reverence—that is to say, reverence properly so called — for something altogether different.

Take the following passage from Mr Lecky's 'History of European Morals.'[2] "There are several influences which, as civilisation advances, diminish the spirit of reverence among mankind. Reverence is one of those feelings which in rationalistic systems would occupy at best a very ambiguous position; for it is extremely questionable whether the great evils which have grown out of it, in the form of religious superstition and political servitude, have not made it a source of

---

[1] In so far as they call forth emotion. See pp. 100, 111, 112.
[2] Vol. i. p. 141.

more unhappiness than happiness. Yet however doubtful may be its position if estimated by its bearing on happiness and on progress, there are few persons who are not conscious that no character can attain a supreme degree of excellence in which the reverential spirit is wanting. . . . The habits of advancing civilisation are, if I mistake not, on the whole inimical to its growth. For reverence grows out of a sense of constant dependence. It is fostered by that condition of religious thought in which men believe that each incident that befalls them is directly and specially ordained, and every event is therefore fraught with moral import. It is fostered by that condition of scientific knowledge in which every portentous natural phenomenon is supposed to be the result of a direct divine interpretation, and awakens in consequence emotions of humility and awe. It is fostered in that stage of political life when loyalty and reverence for the sovereign is the dominating passion; when the aristocracy branching forth from the throne spreads habits of deference and subordination through every village; when a revolutionary, a democratic, and a sceptical spirit are alike unknown. Every great change, either of belief or of circumstances, brings with it a change of emotions. . . . Benevolence, uprightness, enterprise, intellectual honesty, a love of freedom and a hatred of superstition, are growing around us; but we look in vain for that most beautiful character of the past, so distrustful of self, so trustful of others, so simple, so modest, so devout, which, even when Ixion-like it bestowed its affections upon a cloud, made its very illusions the source of some of the purest virtues of our nature. In a few minds, the contemplation of the sublime order of nature produces a reverential feeling; but to the great majority of mankind, it is an incontestable though mournful fact, that the discovery of controlling and unchanging law deprives the phenomena of their moral significance; and nearly all the social and political spheres in which reverence was fostered have passed away. . . . A superstitious age, like every other phase of human history, has its distinctive virtues, which must necessarily decline before a new stage of progress can be attained."

This, it seems to me, represents fairly well the

common view in regard to reverence,—a view which I consider to be fundamentally erroneous and thoroughly mischievous. Mr Lecky, you will observe, asserts that the ages of superstition were pre-eminently the ages of reverence—that, in fact, reverence and superstition diminish and increase together. He asserts that reverence grows out of a sense of dependence; and that this sense of dependence, on the one hand, is fostered by a belief in the disorderliness and capriciousness of nature, and on the other hand leads to a tacit acquiescence in social degradation and political servitude. He asserts that, on the whole, it is more than likely reverence has a tendency to produce unhappiness rather than happiness; and yet at the same time he admits "no character can obtain the supreme degree of excellence in which a reverential spirit is wanting."

Now with all these assertions, except the last, I most entirely disagree; and I maintain that if the last assertion be true—" no character can obtain the supreme degree of excellence in which a reverential spirit is wanting"—if that assertion be true, all the others *must be* false. The reason why Mr Lecky does not see this is that he uses the word "reverence," as it is so often used in common life, for two totally different things. In the one sense of the word, which I believe is the true sense, reverence is the very antithesis of superstition; they diminish and increase inversely. In this sense of the term, reverence does not grow out of a sense of dependence—has nothing whatever to do with it. It is not fostered by belief in the disorderliness of nature, but on the contrary by a recognition of the reign of law. It does not lead to a tacit acquiescence in social degradation and political servitude; but on the contrary it would stimulate every one who possessed it to strive for political and social reform. It does not, it never has, it never can, lead to misery; but on the contrary, though it is not directly connected with happiness or unhappiness, its tendency indirectly is always and necessarily towards the increase of happiness. And lastly, the conditions of the present age are peculiarly conducive to reverence. Never since the world began was there so much reverence as there is to-day. Let us see. Let us ask what is the proper signification of the word.

Our idea of reverence will vary with, and depend upon, our idea of religion, since God, or the gods, have been universally regarded as the especial objects of reverence. Now there are two kinds of religion—the older and barbaric form, based upon fear; the modern and civilised form, based upon love. People used to think that religion consisted in doing what was necessary to secure the complaisance of a supernatural power or powers, without whose complaisance they would have a bad time in this world and the next. There are some people even yet for whom religion means nothing more. But the best men in all ages have understood by religion, the worship of that which, apart from all reference to consequences, *deserved* to be worshipped. Mr Lecky seems to aim at combining the two views. But they never can be combined; they are contradictory. Just as we must choose between the alternative forms of religion, so we must choose between the alternative forms of reverence,—between that which is based upon fear, and that which is based upon love. They are incompatible—absolutely. We cannot at the same time take both. We cannot love that which we are afraid of; we cannot be afraid of that which we love. "Perfect love casteth out fear." And just because in the present age the old superstitious form of reverence is dying out, it follows the way is being prepared for the other form, which alone deserves the name.

The lower animals are by general consent supposed to be incapable of reverence; but if the sentiment grew, as Mr Lecky says it does, out of the sense of dependence, then the brute creation must be pre-eminently distinguished for it. The dog, whose master has beaten him, has a very keen sense of dependence, and so have the poultry that the dairymaid is feeding; but we should never dream of saying that the dog assumed a reverential attitude, or that the poultry approached the dairymaid reverentially.

If fear could give rise to reverence, a belief in the disorderliness of nature would, as Mr Lecky asserts, foster the spirit of reverence. When men knew little or nothing of natural law, they felt themselves the abject slaves of nature. They thought that they were at the mercy of a host of forces, which at any moment might conspire to torment or destroy them. But the dread with which this thought impressed them was not reverence. It was no more reverence than the feeling with which the garotter regards the cat-o'-nine tails. Religion, in the time of Lucretius, meant belief in the capricious interference of bad-tempered deities; and it was the aim of that illustrious poet to make men disbelieve in the gods, and so to free their minds from dread. Religion, in one celebrated passage, Lucretius represents as standing with angry mien over the terrified form of prostrate Humanity. Lucretius did a great, and (paradoxical as it may sound) a religious, work. In helping to destroy the old superstitious dread, he at the same time helped to pave the way for real, genuine reverence. Those old gods were despicable; and it was irreverent not to despise them.

If, once more, the sentiment of reverence were an abject sentiment, then no doubt it would have been fostered, as Mr Lecky says it was, by the old-fashioned notions about the throne and the nobility, by the old-fashioned belief in the "right divine of kings to govern wrong," and such a belief would of course lead to social degradation and political servitude. But this kind of belief, and this kind of feeling, is quite incompatible with a reverence that has its root in love.

If, again, reverence be, as Mr Lecky seems to think, synonymous with dread, then no doubt everything that tended to foster reverence tended at the same time to increase the misery of mankind. But if the true reverence be akin to love, then the substitution of reverence for the old superstitious dread must manifestly increase human happiness. "Fear hath torment."

If, finally, reverence springs from fear of a power or powers that will hurt us, then Mr Lecky is right in saying that the conditions of our age are incompatible with its development. But if, on the contrary, reverence has its root in love, if it involves admiration—admiration for that which is pre-eminently admirable—then the conditions of our age are in its favour; this may be called *par excellence* the age of reverence.

Manifestly the word reverence is best adapted to express the sentiment of the soul for that which is pre-eminently admirable. Except in cases of what is falsely called religion, we should never dream of applying the term to that which we fear. We should never speak of revering an earthquake, of revering a murderer, of revering the devil; but if the power to do us harm were a sufficient claim to reverence, there would be nothing inappropriate in so doing. How it was that the word came to be applied, in so-called religions, to objects of fear, I will explain to you another day. For the present it is sufficient to point out that "reverence" naturally suggests to us admiration rather than terror; and this notwithstanding all misleading associations to the contrary. We are conscious of no incongruity when we speak of revering a saint, of revering a reformer, of revering a philanthropist, of revering our Father in heaven. Mr Lecky has told us—and in this statement we shall all concur—that no character can attain the supreme degree of excellence in which the reverential spirit is wanting. Now the *true* object of reverence is the object which such a character reveres. And what is that? What is it that such a character regards as highest and best? What is it that such a character supremely admires and loves? It is goodness.

Reverence, then, I define as the devotion of the soul to goodness. It implies, as I have said, admiration, but it is more than admiration. It implies love, but it is more than love. It is self-surrender, consecration, devotion.

I will give you two illustrations. The one is contained in a poem of Lowell's. You remember the old classic legend about Prometheus. This pre-historic hero was said to have taught mankind the use of fire, and made them acquainted with architecture, mathematics, writing, medicine, navigation, and other arts and sciences. In all this he had been acting contrary to the will of Zeus, who in a fit of anger chained him to a rock, and sent an eagle to prey perpetually on his vitals. Prometheus remained undaunted, and refused to acknowledge himself in the wrong. The poet represents him as addressing to Zeus a passionate expostulation :—

> "Why art thou made a god of, thou poor type
> Of anger and revenge and cunning force?
> True power was never born of brutish strength.
> There is a higher purity than thou,
> And higher purity is greater strength.
> Thy nature is thy doom, at which thy heart
> Trembles behind the thick wall of thy might.
> Let man but will, and thou art god no more."

Of course that is only legend; but the legend was "written for our learning." Prometheus is the impersonation of the true spirit of reverence. He will do all the good he can, whatever happens to himself. He will not, for the sake of avoiding pain, say that right is wrong or that wrong is right. He remains always firm to his conviction of the paramount value of goodness and of its ultimate and absolute triumph.

The other illustration I take from John Stuart Mill's 'Examination of Sir William Hamilton's Philosophy.' Mill is arguing against the view that such words as Love, Justice, and the like, when applied to God, must be understood in a different sense from that which they bear in relation to man. "I take my stand," he says, "upon the acknowledged principle of logic and of morality, that when we mean different things, we have no right to call them by the same name. Language has no meaning for the words Just, Merciful, Benevolent, Good, save that in which we predicate them of our fellow-creatures; and unless that is what we intend to express by them, we have no business to employ them. . . . If in ascribing goodness to God, I do not mean the goodness of which I have some knowledge, but an incomprehensible attribute of an incomprehensible substance, which, for aught I know, may be a totally different quality from that which I love and venerate — what do I mean by calling it goodness? and what reason have I for venerating it? If I know nothing about what the attribute is, I cannot tell that it is a proper object of veneration. To say that God's goodness may be different in kind from man's goodness, what is it but saying, with a slight change of phraseology, that God may possibly not be good? . . . If, instead of the glad tidings that there is a Being in whom all the excellencies which the highest human mind can conceive exist in a degree inconceivable to us, I am informed that the world is ruled by a Being whose attributes are infinite, but what they are we cannot learn, nor what are the principles of His government, except that the highest human morality which we are capable of conceiving does not sanction them,—convince me of it, and I will bear my fate as I may. But when I am told I must believe this, and at the same time call this Being by the names which express and affirm the highest human morality, I say in plain terms I will not! Whatever power such a Being may have over me, there is one thing he shall not do—he shall not compel me to worship him. I will call no being good who is not what I mean when I apply that epithet to my fellow-creatures. And if such a Being can send me to hell for not so calling him, to hell I will go." I am acquainted with nothing nobler in the literature of the world. It expresses the highest conceivable reverence—the reverence of a man who would willingly endure for ever the torments of the damned, rather than be for a moment disloyal to that which he regards as good.

You will observe that there is nothing degrading about this devotion of the soul to goodness.

It has been well said that "on earth there is nothing great but man, and in man there is nothing great but mind." I think we may add that in mind there is nothing great but goodness. In comparison with this all else is little. Goodness is the one thing in the universe that deserves our homage. He who renders that homage does not thereby demean himself; he demeans himself only by withholding it. There is nothing that exalts a man so much as reverence. Our place in the scale of being is determined by the intensity of our devotion to what is good. The highest type of man is the man in whom the reverential spirit is most developed. Reverence is not cringing; it is aspiration. It is not the prostration of the body before a power that repels; it is the elevation of the spirit to a goodness that attracts. We become noble just in proportion as we yield to this attractive influence. Devotion to goodness will make us in a sense divine. When that devotion is constant and complete, we shall be perfect, "as He is perfect," good even as that absolute goodness which we are accustomed to call "God."

Reverence.

II.

THE DIFFERENCE BETWEEN REVERENCE AND RESPECT.

MR LECKY asserts that reverence springs from a sense of dependence, that it is fostered by superstition, by political servitude, by everything which tends to make us conscious of dependence, and that, since the conditions which were most favourable to it are now passing away, the spirit of reverence is actually on the wane. I pointed out to you that all these assertions were demonstrably false. The fact is, he confuses reverence with dread. True reverence—reverence properly so called—has its root not in fear but in love. The feeling of reverence has nothing whatever to do with the feeling of dependence. The latter, the feeling of dependence, is strong in the lower animals; and yet in them the former, the feeling of reverence, is, by common consent, always absent. The dog, whom we feed and flog, has a very lively sense of dependence; but we should not imagine that he is manifesting a spirit of reverence when he stands hopefully upon his hind legs, or tremblingly puts his tail between them. Nor do we ever in common life say that we ourselves revere anything of which we are afraid. We do not, for instance, imagine that we revere a man, simply because we should be frightened to meet him in a dark lane. There is one thing, and one thing only, to which the word reverence properly and naturally applies—viz., goodness. We can speak without any impropriety—we do sometimes speak —of revering those who are supremely and in a rare degree good. In proportion as a man rises above the level of the savage, he comes to feel that goodness is the most admirable, the most lovable, the most desirable thing in the universe. All this—admiration, love, desire—is implied in the word reverence, which may therefore be defined as the devotion of the soul to goodness. And I said further, that the conditions of the present age, so far from being incompatible with the sentiment of reverence, are distinctly in its favour. We should have expected, *à priori*, that this highest sentiment of the soul would become more intense during the progress of evolution. And so it has. Science, in diminishing our fear of nature, makes it at any rate *possible* for us to reverence the Creator. We have got rid of the old superstitious belief in the "divine right" of kings, but we are all the more ready to reverence them for their actual goodness. In point of fact, real goodness, wherever it exists, is more valued by a larger number of persons in the present than in the past. This is emphatically the age of reverence.

To-day I shall be mainly occupied in explaining the difference between reverence and respect. And, first of all, you will observe that you may often respect what you do not and cannot reverence. We may respect men, for instance, on account of their ability; but it is impossible on that ground alone to revere them. You would never think of saying that you revered a mathematician or an opera singer *as such*. We may respect men again on account of their position; but there is nothing in mere position to revere. A king, a judge, a professor, are to be treated with respect, — there is a certain dignity and authority attaching to their offices; but no one in his senses would think of revering them if their characters were bad. The clergy, as you know, have appropriated the word "Reverend" as their official title. Now in my judgment this is a mistake. There is indeed a measure of respect due to a clergyman on account of the office which he holds, but in a clergyman *as such* there is nothing reverend. If you are to revere him, it can only be on account of his goodness; and a layman deserves just as much reverence, if he be equally good. However, the word "Reverend," as applied to the clergy, has long since become a matter of mere convention; its etymological meaning is no longer remembered. When you are addressing an envelope, and put the mystic letters "Rev." before a name, you have no more intention of revering the man than if you put the letters "Esq." after. That the clergy as a whole are more remarkable for goodness than any other respectable class of citizens, I for one do not believe. But even if they were, mark you, this would not give the individual clergyman any title to be revered. It is as true of the clergy as of the laity, that they can have but one quality deserving of reverence, viz., the quality of goodness.—That is one point of difference between reverence and respect: you may often respect what you cannot and should not revere.

Here is another difference. Respect can be simulated, reverence cannot. There are various ways of showing respect. For instance, some people show it by taking off the hat, others by putting it on; some by removing their shoes, others by hanging down their heads; some by a bow or a curtsey, others by complete prostration; some by clasping their hands, others by putting dust on their foreheads, others by a humble expression of countenance; and so on, and so on. Now all these outward signs of respect may be assumed for a purpose, when there is nothing in the mind or heart that corresponds. A boy, for instance, may be apparently respectful to his schoolmaster, because he knows he will be whipped if he is not. But reverence cannot be put on. It is an inward feeling *for which there exists no outward sign.* It of course involves respect, but it is something more, something very different; and for this something more, for this something different, there is no physical expression. Reverence is the surrender of the spirit to the attractive influence of goodness. There is but one way in which a man can manifest it, and that is by becoming himself good.

There is yet another point of difference between reverence and respect. It is possible to respect the wrong objects, or to respect them in the wrong way; but there is no such thing as a mistaken reverence.

For instance, those to whose judgment or authority we decide to submit, are said to be the objects of our respect; and here it is very easy to make a mistake. Look at the old-fashioned respect for the opinions of our ancestors, which was based upon a fallacy. It used to be argued that, as the father is wiser, generally speaking, than the child, so our ancestors must be wiser than we. It was assumed, you see, that the wisest person was the one who was born first. But this is not what makes the father wiser. The father's wisdom results from his being older, and having therefore had more experience. Now manifestly we have had more experience than our ancestors. Much of their experience we inherit unconsciously; and with the rest of it we may by reading make ourselves definitely acquainted. Hence it will be an eternal shame to us if we are not wiser, far wiser, than they. Any honest, earnest thinker of the nineteenth century deserves more respect than a thinker of the first or third. It is more likely that his opinions will be correct. It will be safer for us to submit ourselves to his judgment. We have heard quite enough about the authority of the ancients; it is time we heard something about the authority of the moderns. However, that is merely by the way. I merely wanted to illustrate the fact that it is very easy for us to respect the wrong objects, or to respect the right objects unduly; to give most to those who deserve least, and to give least to those who deserve most. But with regard to reverence—real, genuine reverence—we cannot possibly go wrong. It is a sentiment which we simply cannot feel for anything that is not good. We may, of course, say we feel it: it is quite possible, quite easy, to lie. We may even persuade ourselves that we feel it, when we do not: we have a wonderful power of self-deception. But we cannot really reverence an unworthy object; for reverence is a sentiment which is only called into existence by supreme worth. Goodness, goodness of a high degree, is at once the only thing which deserves reverence, and the only thing which ever can be reverenced.

"If that be so," I hear some one object, "how is it that men in all ages have revered deities who were bad?" I reply, men never did. Never. The truth of this assertion you will recognise at once if you distinguish between action and feeling, between the outward signs of fear and the inner sentiment of reverence. In all low forms of what is called religion, the deities were regarded as objects of terror. A very large proportion of the human race may be truly said

"To fear their God as though He were a wolf."

Now men cannot reverence an object of terror, however much they may persist in calling Him "God." For reverence implies, as we have seen, admiration and love. But just because they cannot reverence Him—mark you, *just because* they cannot reverence Him—they can and do endeavour to propitiate and bribe Him. They believe that He may be induced, for a consideration, to do them good instead of harm. Sometimes men treat their gods with absolute disrespect. The negro of New Guinea beats his deities when they turn a deaf ear to his request. But as a rule the gods are treated with a great *show* of respect, notwithstanding the poor estimation in which they are held by their worshippers. Why? The reason is this. All the worst qualities of human nature have been ascribed to the hearers and the answerers of prayer; and they were therefore generally conceived of as extraordinarily vain and inordinately fond of flattery. They required their devotees to cringe to them. They had not only to be paid for the benefits they were asked to confer, but they must be paid in a deferential and servile manner. They demanded full acknowledgment of their power to cause misery, before they could be induced to make any one, even for a moment, happy. But this cowardly pandering to the pride of the gods cannot be called reverence. It was not prompted by any love for goodness. It arose simply out of selfishness and fear. And long after the gods have become moderately respectable—long after they are regarded as on the whole superior to average humanity—they are still cultivated, chiefly, and very often simply, for what can be got out of them. Religion, properly so called, cannot exist till a late stage in the development of the race. There is no real religion until the Deity is conceived of as infinitely good, and worshipped upon that ground alone. All early religions—so-called—are distinctly irreligious, and all the outward signs of fear or of respect manifested by their worshippers are distinctly irreverent. Reverence is a devotion to goodness, not a bargaining with evil. Nothing can be more irreverent than to pretend to worship that which is not good.

You have seen Cologne Cathedral? Nothing more impressive was ever produced by the hand of man. As you stand by the west door, you look down through a long vista of pillars, which seem to stretch away into infinity; and the high altar at the end appears the very Shechinah of Omnipotence. If you approach the altar and remain near it for a little, you will notice a number of persons passing it by with a nod of the head—a rude, familiar, almost insulting nod. Afterwards, when you walk round the cathedral, you will come to an obscure corner, in which stands a small shrine to the Virgin, who is represented by a child's doll, bedecked with tawdry finery. If you wait a little you will see some of those very persons who passed the altar with a nod, lying flat upon the ground before that paltry shrine. Now, what do you suppose is the meaning of this? How is it that men nod to the altar and fall prostrate before the doll? I will tell you. But first let me give you another illustration of the same kind, taken from a poem of Rossetti's, called "The Last Confession." The speaker is relating the story of his life to a priest.

He is talking about himself and the girl he loved:—

> "We dwelt at Monza, far away from home,
> If home we had; and in the Duomo there
> I sometimes entered with her when she prayed.
> An image of our Lady stands there, wrought
> In marble by some great Italian hand,
> In the great days when she and Italy
> Sat on one throne together; and to her—
> And to none else—my loved one told her heart.
> She was a woman then; and as she knelt,
> Her sweet brow in the sweet brow's shadow there,
> They seemed two kindred forms, whereby our land
> Made manifest herself in womanhood.
> Father, the day I speak of was the first
> For weeks that I had borne her company
> Into the Duomo: and these weeks had been
> Much troubled; for then first the glimpses came
> Of some impenetrable restlessness,
> Growing in her to make her changed and cold.
> And as we entered there that day, I bent
> My eyes on the fair image, and I said
> Within my heart, 'Oh, turn her heart to me!'
> And so I left her to her prayers, and went
> To gaze upon the pride of Monza's shrine,
> Where in the sacristy the light still falls
> Upon the iron crown of Italy.
> . . . .
> But coming back, I wondered when I saw
> That the sweet Lady of her prayers now stood
> Alone without her; until farther off,
> Before some new Madonna, gaily decked,

> Tinselled and gewgawed, a slight German toy,
> I saw her kneel, still praying. At my step
> She rose, and side by side we left the church.
> I was much moved, and sharply questioned her
> On her transferred devotion ; but she seemed
> Stubborn and heedless ; till she lightly laughed,
> And said, ' The old Madonna ? Ay, indeed,
> She had my old thoughts,—this one has my new !' "

What is the explanation of the worship of dolls ? Why this. The object of our worship will be determined by our character. The girl of Rossetti's poem transferred her devotion only after she had exchanged her innocence for guilt. She could not, she dared not, present herself before the old Madonna, whose marble statue typified purity, dignity, all that is most divine ; but the tawdry doll represented a being in harmony with her own degraded nature, who might be prevailed upon to connive at sin. And so with the doll in Cologne Cathedral. No one could possibly respect, much less revere, the being whom it represents. But that is the very reason why it has so many worshippers. It looks so fickle, so vain, so corruptible, that they make sure of getting something out of it by means of flattery and bribes. Whereas the altar symbolises an unchanging and unchangeable Being, of infinite power, but of infinite majesty, who has no sympathy with what is mean or petty, and who is too wise to answer a foolish prayer; a Being whose very essence is goodness, and whose one eternal purpose is that we should become likewise good; a Being in whose presence we are conscious of no want but the hunger and thirst after righteousness, to whom we dare not offer any petitions but such as may be summed up in the words, "Thy will be done."

What kind of deity is it that you are accustomed to worship? Is your god symbolised by the altar or by the doll?

Reverence.

III.

CRITICISMS.

We all of us employ language in a more or less loose style, and we should generally be puzzled to give, on the spur of the moment, a definition of nine-tenths of the terms we use. Now there is no harm in our employing any word in any sense, provided we explain to our hearers or readers the signification which we propose to attach to it, and provided we ourselves always strictly adhere to this signification. It is desirable, however, to conform as far as possible to the common and popular usage, or else we shall oblige people not only to learn a number of new definitions, but also to unlearn a number of old ones. Suppose, for example, I wrote a mathematical treatise, in which I defined a triangle as a four-sided figure enclosed by four straight lines, and a square as a three-sided figure contained by three straight lines. Here I should be reversing old definitions for no purpose, and simply wasting the reader's time and attention. The words square and triangle were long ago defined once and for ever, and any change in the definition would be a change for the worse. But you will see the case is quite different with words like religion, worship, reverence. These terms stand not for simple, but for very complex ideas. The attempt to define them with any approach to accuracy has seldom, if ever, been made. They are constantly used in a variety of senses. And it becomes necessary for us, therefore, to determine which of these significations is the best. To do this satisfactorily we must begin by observing the way in which the term is generally used. This will give us the fundamental idea involved in it, and the fundamental idea will lead us to the true definition. When we have got so far, we shall probably be able to explain how it is that the term is sometimes used improperly in other and conflicting senses. This is what I have been attempting to do with regard to the subject of reverence.

Some criticisms have been offered to me during the past week, to which I must now refer. It is said that "reverence" must have originally implied fear, for it is allied etymologically to the word wary. It was first used when the gods were conceived of as cruel and ill-disposed. In those days the word reverence signified fear of evil that repelled. How then, it is asked, can I be justified in saying that the fundamental idea of reverence is love for goodness that attracts? I will explain. You must distinguish between the fundamental idea and the original idea. The fundamental conception implied in a word at any given time may be something different, and may indeed be something quite opposed, to the conception which was originally implied in it. The old term may have come to be the best expression for an entirely new idea. The German word *schlecht* once meant good, afterwards good for nothing, and now stands for what is positively bad. Our word prevent, which now means to hinder, formerly meant to help. And a change no less extreme has taken place in the signification of the words religion and reverence.

"Religion" originally meant paying court to supernatural powers, who were naturally inclined to injure us, but who might be bribed into letting us alone, or perhaps even into giving us good things. The word *cult*—one of the synonyms for religion—is very suggestive. It is derived, as you know, from *colo*, which meant primarily to till the soil, and secondarily to pay attention to the gods. In olden time men cultivated the deities just as they did their estates—for the sake of what could be got out of them. We still speak of cultivating a useful acquaintance—*i.e.*, paying attention to a person who has it in his power to give us something in return. But such an "attention" to the gods is now generally called superstition. The term religion has come, or is coming, to mean the worship of a Being who is not evilly disposed, but on the contrary infinitely good; the worship of a Being, not for what can be got out of Him, but simply and solely for what He is in Himself.

And a similar change has passed over the word reverence. No doubt it once meant the prudent and politic cultivation of the gods. That was the original idea implied in it. But that is not the fundamental idea to-day. We never apply the term in common life to anything which we fear. However much we might do to propitiate a garotter, a scandal-monger, or a fiend, we should never speak of reverencing them. Whereas it would not be at all unnatural or illegitimate to speak of the reverence of a man for the woman whom he loved. Manifestly then the term reverence in the present day implies fundamentally, not fear for something which repels, but love for something which attracts. And this attractive something I explained to you was goodness. We admire beauty, we respect ability, but we revere only character. The devotion of the soul to goodness is, or at any rate is becoming, the meaning of the word reverence.

And you will find, if you look into the matter, that when the word is used in other senses, it is only through misleading associations and a consequent confusion of thought. For example: though no one would think of saying that men ever revered wickedness, it might be said, without the impropriety of the expression being at once apparent, that men had sometimes revered wicked gods. Such an expression is really a contradiction in terms, and therefore absurd. But we are prevented from perceiving immediately that it is ludicrous, owing to the associations connected in our mind with the word god. This term now suggests to us a good being. There can be no such thing therefore as a bad god strictly speaking, for that would be equivalent to a bad-good being. A wicked being is not properly called a god. When he is so called, it is *implied* that there is something in him to revere; and if there were, he would be good.

There is another very common source of confusion in this matter. Because it is sometimes possible to respect and revere the same person, it comes to be imagined that respect and reverence are synonymous. But they are not. We respect the opinions of a scientific expert, because we believe that on certain subjects they are likely to be more correct than our own. And our respect for his judgment is not at all determined by his moral character. But we should never dream of saying that we revered him, if his character were notoriously bad. It would be impossible even to imagine that we revered him, unless his character were pre-eminently good. Since then it depends entirely on a man's character whether reverence is given or denied him, it follows that the object of reverence is goodness, and goodness alone. Any other use of the word is now illegitimate.

The second criticism I have received is this. You remember I told you that it was impossible to reverence wrongly; that you could not reverence any one unless he deserved it, or more than he deserved. For reverence, I said, was a sentiment which was only called forth in us by goodness of a rare and supreme kind, and about goodness there can be no mistake. Now I am asked, "How can this be? since men's notions of goodness vary. Some persons, for example, think it right to allow their parents to die a natural death and then to bury them; others think it their duty to kill their parents prematurely and then to eat them." To this objection I reply that my correspondent is confusing goodness with rightness. The latter is a quality of actions; the former is a quality of character. We do not revere actions; we approve of them or disapprove of them as the case may be: but it is only character we revere. Men's notions of the rightness and wrongness of actions do differ; but their notion of goodness does not, for by goodness is meant the general bent or set of the character. Now there is no possibility of mistaking a man who does upon the whole what pleases him and what he thinks will pay, for a man who upon the whole does what he believes to be right, whether it pays him or not—nay, even when it involves him in loss, agony or death. There is no possibility of mistaking a man whose character is essentially bad for a man whose character is good enough to be revered.

There is one other criticism to which I must reply. I was very hard, it is said, upon the worshippers of the old gods, whose "religion" consisted mainly in sacrificial bribes, and upon those persons in the present day whose prayers are mainly devoted to asking the Deity for physical and temporal blessings. Now it was not I who was hard upon them, but the nature of things. I was merely stating a fact. And facts generally are hard; it is quite out of my power to soften them. The fact which I was trying to elucidate is a particularly stubborn one. It is well enough understood in some connections; and it has been my one sole aim in preaching these sermons to make it apparent in connection with the subject of reverence. The fact in question is simply this, that you cannot be doing two contradictory things at one and the same time. I said there was no religion in selfish prayer. Nor is there. There cannot be. Religion is the worship of goodness; and every prayer therefore that has anything to do with religion may be summed up in the words "Thy will be done." Mind you, I don't say anything against other and inferior prayers. Christ Himself offered them. It is natural, inevitable, that if we believe in a God, we should make known to Him *all* our requests. But we may do so day after day, month after month, year after year, and never have once come within the sphere of religion. Prayer of any kind no doubt implies certain theological beliefs. But the only prayer that implies religion is the prayer for goodness. Our prayers for health or money or pleasure need not be distinctly anti-religious; but they will be even that, unless we are willing to conclude them with the words—" Nevertheless, not as I will, but as Thou wilt." The desire for enjoyment, though natural enough and often harmless enough, is not a religious desire. It has nothing to do with goodness. And there is always a danger that it may lead us into positive irreligion, that it may induce us implicitly to sum up our prayers by saying, Nevertheless, not as Thou wilt, but as I will. But in any case it is absurd to suppose ourselves religious when we are only trying to get what we want. A schoolboy might as well plume himself on his filial affection, because he was always writing to his father for pocket-money. There is a kind of "religion" which has been very happily termed other-worldliness. It consists simply in doing whatever may be thought necessary to make the next life pleasant, in trying to get to heaven merely because that is regarded as a more comfortable place than hell. There is another kind of "religion," which might perhaps be termed hyper-worldliness. It consists exclusively in invoking the aid of supernatural power to enhance the enjoyments of the present life. But neither other-worldliness nor hyper-worldliness has anything to do with religion in the true acceptation of the term. It is a fact, an unalterable fact—hard if you like, but you must not blame me for its hardness—that "cultivating" a powerful Being for the sake of what you can get from Him, is not the same thing as worshipping a good Being for the sake of what He is in Himself; asking God to give you things is not the same as giving yourself to God. Reverence —of which worship is the highest and intensest form—reverence is the devotion of the soul to goodness. There is but one way of showing it: we must surrender ourselves to the attractive influence of goodness and become ourselves good. The prayer of real religion is the expression of this surrender. For instance—

> "I do not ask, O Lord, that life may be
>   A pleasant road;
> I do not ask that Thou wouldst take from me
>   Aught of its load.

I do not ask that flowers should always spring
   Beneath my feet ;
I know too well the poison and the sting
   Of things too sweet.

For one thing only, Lord, dear Lord, I plead—
   Lead me aright :
Though strength should falter and though heart should bleed,
   Lead me to Light."

Reverence.

IV.

ITS EVOLUTION.

LET me give you a *résumé* of the ground we have already traversed. According to the popular view, reverence is the outcome of a sense of dependence. This, I have shown you, is not the case. For where the sense of dependence is greatest, the feeling of reverence is altogether absent—as, for example, in a sucking infant. No one would dream of saying that the little creature cried for its bottle reverentially. Again according to the popular view, reverence is fostered and developed by fear; and this view derives a certain plausibility from the fact that the word reverence is connected etymologically with such words as wary and wariness. I have shown you however—with an abundance of illustration which it would be tedious to repeat for those who have gone with me, and useless for those who have not—that except through misleading associations and confusion of thought, we never now apply the term reverence to anything of which we are afraid; that the persons whom we speak of revering do not repel, but on the contrary attract us. In other words, the meaning of the term reverence has been completely changed. I also explained to you that a similar change had occurred in the signification of the word religion. In early times the deities were generally regarded as ill-disposed beings, bent on injuring men. Religion *then* meant doing whatever may be necessary, in the way of sacrifices and all sorts of bribes, to avert their ill-will and to induce them to bestow on their worshippers pleasant things instead of unpleasant. But the noblest and best amongst us in the present day conceive of the Deity as infinitely good; and when they speak of worship they mean the reverence given to Him on account of what He is in Himself, and not for any ulterior and selfish motive.

Now we must make our choice between these alternative views. We can no more combine them than we can walk backwards and forwards at the same time. The accepted derivation of the word religion is from *religere,* to attend to.[1] When the word was invented, men attended to the gods from selfish motives, for the sake of what they expected the gods to give them. And it was this selfish kind of attention which was at first signified by the term religion. But now the word has come, or is coming, to mean unselfish attention,—self-surrendering devotion. And if we use it in this sense, we must use it exclusively in this sense; for the two meanings are contradictory, and one word can therefore no more stand for both than the same sign in algebra could stand for plus and minus. Selfish attention to the gods we may call other-worldliness, hyper-worldliness, superstition,—we may call it anything we please except religion. If we are not satisfied with the

---

[1] Our word negligent, I may remind the reader, comes from the same root, but with a negation prefixed.

word now in existence, we must coin a new one. But if we want our language to convey ideas, if we wish to effect any rational purposes with it, we must give up the effort to make one and the same term stand for two totally different things, —for a selfish truckling with power, and an unselfish devotion to goodness.

Now I am asked, "If reverence be devotion to goodness, and only that,—if religion be the worship of goodness, and only that,—how can this new religion be an evolution from the old?" My answer is, the new is not an evolution from the old. That we should ever have been inclined, even for a moment, to think it was, affords a remarkable illustration of what Bacon calls the idols of the market-place. Bacon, as some of you know, classified the causes or sources of error under four heads, which he called idols. The word idol means literally an image, and then a false appearance or a sham that may be readily mistaken for reality. By idols, therefore, Bacon meant the delusive appearances that lead men into error. One set of idols—one of the four classes—he calls idols of the market-place, and by this he meant the delusiveness of words. The language in which we communicate our ideas is full of false appearances; and the consequence is that we often produce fallacies when we think we are making syllogisms. There is no more common source of fallacy, *e.g.*, than the fact that the same word is frequently made to do duty for totally different things. We are apt to fancy that, if two things are represented by the same word, they must be identical, or similar, or at any rate intimately connected with one another in the way of evolution or otherwise. Of course there are certain cases where we should never be taken in. No one, for example, would ever dream of supposing that the drum of the ear was an evolutionary development from the musical instrument of the same name, or that the sum of £25 owed its existence to an animal of an equine nature because it is sometimes called a " pony." That is a kind of mistake into which there is not much danger of our falling. When, however, a word like religion has been used with unbroken continuity for centuries and millenniums of years, it is not to be wondered at if we are at first inclined to suppose, that all the objects to which the term has been applied are necessarily connected with one another in the way of evolutionary descent. But there is no earthly necessity about it. Whether as a matter of fact they have been so connected, can only be discovered by an examination of the objects themselves. There may be a hundred reasons why things are called by the same name besides that of evolutionary connection. And when we come to compare the new religion with the old, we find that they are as opposed and disconnected as it is possible for any two things in this universe to be.

One of my correspondents asks: "Admitting that religion in the true acceptation of the term is, as you define it, the worship of goodness, would you not go on to say that all other faiths and aspirations are necessary steps in the evolution of religion?" To this I reply, it depends on what you mean by "faiths and aspirations." If you mean aspirations after pleasant things, and faith in the power of certain persons to give the things, I answer most emphatically—No. Such aspirations and such faith, so far from being stepping-stones to religion, were the greatest possible obstacles in its way. Selfish attention to the gods is not only inferior to, but is the very antithesis of, unselfish attention. The desire for pleasure will no more evolve into the love of goodness, than a taste for ferns will evolve into a passion for mathematics.

Another of my correspondents writes as follows: "It seems to me you demand something like a perfect moral development in us, before we are capable of reverence. But is this possible? Must not reverence, like everything else, have had a beginning?" Now it is true I did say reverence was concerned with goodness of a rare and supreme kind. But of course the standard of goodness will vary from age to age. At one time the man who refrains from theft and from murder will be regarded as a prodigy of self-control, will be looked upon as extraordinarily good, and may even come to be revered as a saint. In another age such an amount of self-control would only suffice to prevent his being hanged. I never dreamed of demanding a "perfect moral development." For the moral development of every finite being is, and will always be, imperfect. There is probably less difference morally between you and a savage, than between yourself to-day and yourself ten thousand years hence. As to reverence. "having had a beginning," of course it had. But if reverence, as we now understand it, means unselfish devotion to goodness, why, in the name of logic, should you suppose that it had its beginning in a selfish bargaining with evil?

The same correspondent further asks: "Do you not think one might have a low ideal of God, and yet be sincere in reverencing Him? I cannot help thinking that you limited the use of the term religion, in the same way as that of reverence, until only a perfect religion can claim the name at all. But is not the most imperfect and rudimentary religion, so long as it includes *any* love and admiration for what is at all good or better than oneself, or *any* effort to be better, still religion?" Certainly. That is precisely what I have been trying to show. Any love and admiration for what is at all good or better than oneself, any effort to be better—however rudimentary and imperfect—is religion. But love and admiration for pleasant things, and efforts to acquire them—however refined, however excusable, however legitimate—are not religion, and unless kept in check, soon pass into irreligion. The fault I find with the devotees of the older religions is not that their ideal of goodness was low, but that the deities they worshipped were for the most part idealisations of badness; not that their attention to the gods showed only a feeble love of goodness, but that it was prompted simply by a desire for pleasure, and not by the love of goodness at all.

So far from the older religions of fear and greed having evolved into anything essentially different from what they originally were, they have scarcely evolved at all. They still exist around us, in essence the same as ever, though some of their accidents, some of their external manifestations, have changed. Look, by way of illustration, at Mrs Quickly's account of the death of Falstaff. "He cried out," she says, "God, God, God, three or four times, and I, to comfort him, bid him he should not think of

God. I hoped there was no need to trouble himself yet with any such thoughts." For many people even now God means merely this — a Being who, if they don't take care, will send them to hell. Upon the whole, the most remarkable feature in the evolution of the older religions is the ever-increasing respect paid to conventionality, to fashion, to Mrs Grundy. These three deities probably never had so many devotees as they have to-day. And what else could you have expected? Can a clean thing come out of an unclean? Evolution can do a great deal, but there is one thing it cannot do — it cannot bring a thing out of its contradictory; it cannot develop something intrinsically and altogether good out of something which is essentially and wholly bad. From religions, the very sacraments of which were selfish, it is absolutely inconceivable that the religion of unselfishness could have been evolved.

But I must ask you to bear in mind, when I call the false religions of fear and greed the old religions, I by no means intend to imply that there has not been any true religion in the world till now. God forbid! Just as the religions which I call old have survived into the present, so we can find traces of the religion which I call new far away back in the remotest past.[1] The conception of religion—as the self-surrendering worship of infinite goodness—is clearer now than formerly; there are more men and women who seek to realise this ideal in the present than there were in the past. But we can discover the dim beginnings of such a religion all through the bygone history of the race. Something like it may occasionally be found even in savage tribes. An old Samoyede woman, being asked by Castren whether she ever said her prayers, replied, "Every morning I step out of my tent and bow before the sun, and say, 'When thou risest, I too rise from my bed.' And every evening I say, 'When thou sinkest down, I too sink down to rest.'" That was an unselfish act of homage. She did not seem to expect anything for her pains. She was content simply to give. And in all the sacred literature of the world we find occasional traces, at least, of a pure and disinter-

[1] See my 'Defects of Modern Christianity,' pp. 182-197.

ested devotion of goodness. Such a devotion may frequently have existed in the hearts of individuals, when the majority of their contemporaries were steeped to the core in selfishness. In all ages there have been men—prophets, philosophers, reformers—who have shown their religiousness by their *opposition* to the religion of their times. Amongst the Jews there was a long line of such teachers, extending over fifteen hundred years. The Hebrew prophets were always protesting against the mercantile religion of the priests. They were always insisting on the irreligiousness of trying to atone for sin and to propitiate Jehovah by sacrificial bribes. "I hate and despise your feast-days. Though ye offer me burnt-offerings and meat-offerings, I will not accept them. Take away from me the noise of your songs; I will not hear the melody of your viols. But let justice run down as water, and righteousness as a mighty stream. Will the Lord be pleased with thousands of rams, and ten thousands of rivers of oil? What doth the Lord require of thee, but to do justly and to love mercy, and to walk humbly with thy God?

The sacrifices of God are a broken spirit and a contrite heart." And there are one or two great names standing out conspicuously in the records of the past, such as Socrates, Zoroaster, Gautama. These men were far advanced, to say the least, towards the true conception of religion. They had no patience with bad ideals. But for that very reason they do not represent the religions of their day. It was their antagonism to these religions that has won them their eternal fame. They were regarded by their fellows as pre-eminently irreligious; not unfrequently, like Socrates and Gautama, they have gone by the name of atheist. You see therefore how very necessary it is, in seeking to trace the history of religion, to be on your guard against the misleading influence of words.

Reverence.

V.

ITS EVOLUTION—(*continued*).

I HAVE defined reverence as the devotion of the soul to goodness. It is only goodness which deserves reverence. Other qualities may be respected, but goodness alone can be revered. And not only *may* goodness be revered, but it has a strange power of *exacting* reverence even from the most depraved. This is finely illustrated in 'The Ring and the Book.' On whom does Guido call for help at the supreme moment? His last appeal is made to his maligned and tortured victim, through whose divine nature he has caught his first glimpse of goodness.

> ". Abate,—Cardinal, Christ, Maria, God,
> *Pompilia*, will you let them murder me?"

Last Sunday I began to discuss the evolution of reverence. This is really the same thing as discussing the evolution of religion. For religion, in the modern acceptation of the term, is the worship of infinite goodness; and worship is but the supreme form of reverence.

This modern conception of religion, we have seen, is something very different, something quite the opposite of the old conception. By religion has always, or almost always, been meant attention to the gods,—some sort of attention. But in the old religions it was generally attention bestowed on objects of which the worshippers were afraid, and was always attention bestowed from selfish motives. Whereas in the new religion it is attention bestowed on the Deity simply because He is good, and not from any desire for self-aggrandisement.

It has been asked—How can this new religion be an evolution from the old? To which my reply was, it cannot be. The only reason for supposing the two opposite kinds of religion to be connected, is the fact that they have both been called religion. This however, as I explained, is no reason at all. Things are often called by the same name through mistake, through inadvertence, and for a host of other reasons besides that of evolutionary development. Though sometimes it is difficult to determine whether one thing is an evolution from another or not, there is one case in which, if we reflect a little, there can be no doubt at all. Nothing is ever an evolution from its contradictory. Now the two kinds of religion—the old and the new—are contradictories. The one is based on fear of evil and on selfish motives. The other is based on love of goodness, and its very essence lies in the unselfishness of its devotion. True religion then—the worship of infinite goodness—did not have its beginning in the fear of bad gods. I propose to show you this morning that it had its origin in the love of good men.

In other words, the evolution of Religion must be distinguished from the history of religions. In the past much has been called religion which was not religion; much has been called atheism and what not, when it was really religion. The evolution of Religion is to be sought, not in the history of churches, but in the history of the human heart. It is there alone that we shall be able to trace the development of Religion in the real sense of that word. We have plenty of histories of religions, but the evolution of Religion is a book which has yet to be written.

It is very important that you should distinguish between evolution and progress. All evolution is progress, but all progress is not evolution. Evolution means the evolving of something higher and better out of something lower and inferior; and this of course is progress. But you may have other kinds of progress. You may have progress where what is superior does not come into existence by means of what is inferior, but in spite of it; where the inferior, instead of being a stage in the development of the superior, is an obstacle which must be overcome before the superior can arise. In the realm of mind progress often results from trying back, from discovering that we were altogether on the wrong path. A change has taken place in men's notion of religion similar to that which occurred in astronomy. The Copernican system was no evolution from the Ptolemaic. The latter system, based on the idea that the sun revolved round the earth, was radically wrong, and could never evolve into anything right. It was necessary that it should be denied, disproved, cast aside. Similarly the love of goodness could never have come out of the fear of evil; nor could unselfish, self-surrendering devotion have been evolved from the self-seeking worship of the older religions.

The fact is, Religion—in the true sense of the word—had its origin in the human affections. "That is not first which is spiritual, but that which is natural; and afterwards that which is spiritual." Worship of infinite goodness is an evolution from reverence for finite goodness. And goodness is but another name for love.

We can trace the dim beginnings of this almost as far back as the dawn of sentient existence; when, for example, a bird voluntarily surrendered her life to save that of her offspring, or when a dog begged off from punishment the child that had been torturing him. And during the course of evolution this love is ever evolving into higher and still higher forms,—into the love of a mother or a sister, into the love of a lover or a friend, into the love of a philanthropist or a reformer, into the love of Gautama or Christ. And all this love, this self-sacrificing goodness, is irresistibly attractive. Love begets love, according to the common proverb. But it does more than that, it begets reverence,—which is the devotion of the soul, the voluntary surrender of the soul, to the attractive influence of goodness. There comes a time when men pass from the actual to the ideal, from the finite to the infinite. Even Christ was limited by the conditions of time and space, so that He Himself said, "My Father is greater than I." There comes a time when we conceive of, or try to conceive of, an infinite impersonation of goodness; and then reverence passes into its supreme and noblest form, which we call worship — the devotion of the soul to God.

All through the history of thought we find that the Creator has sometimes been conceived of as supernaturally and supremely good. I have told you before, how our old Aryan ancestors, even in prehistoric times, must have had a word in their language which meant Heaven-Father,—the word, viz., from which Dyauspitar, Zeupater, and Jupiter are derived. We find the same idea in Plato and elsewhere. And this view was taught with great emphasis and clearness by Christ. But the old unscientific conception of nature prevented its being generally adopted. It could only be a matter of faith,—and faith in spite of what seemed overwhelming evidence to the contrary. So long as men were ignorant of the laws and causes of natural phenomena, ignorant of the fact that these phenomena had any determined laws and causes at all, the Author of nature must inevitably have appeared to the majority of them as capricious and revengeful, as unworthy of confidence or of worship. But now we have reason to believe that the Creator is the same yesterday, to-day, and for ever; for we know that He never interferes with the ordinary course of nature. And this ordinary course of nature,—though it involves much that perplexes us, much for which we cannot altogether account, much which we could have wished otherwise,—is on the whole a cosmos, an orderly and beautiful system, in which, generally speaking, it is happiness to live. The logical inference from nature and her phenomena, from human life and its experiences, to the conception of a beneficent Creator, has been powerfully expressed by Lewis Morris.

" And through all the clear spaces above—O wonder ! O glory of Light !—
Came forth myriads on myriads of worlds, the shining host of the night,—

The vast forces and fires that know the same sun and centre as we ;
The faint planets which roll in vast orbits round suns we shall never see ;

The rays which had sped from the first, with the awful swiftness of light,
To reach only then, it might be, the confines of mortal sight.

O wonder of Cosmical Order ! O Maker and Ruler of all,
Before whose infinite greatness in silence we worship and fall !

Could I doubt that the Will which keeps this great universe steadfast and sure,
Can be less than His creatures thought, full of goodness, pitiful, pure ?

Could I dream that the Power which keeps those great suns
  circling around,
Takes no thought for the humblest life which flutters and falls
  to the ground?

O Faith, thou art higher than all.—Then I turned from the
  glories above,
And from every casement new-lit, there shone a soft radiance
  of love:

Young mothers were teaching their children to fold little hands
  in prayer;
Strong fathers were resting from toil, 'mid the hush of the
  Sabbath air;
Peasant lovers strolled through the lanes, shy and diffident,
  each with each,
Yet knit by some subtle union too fine for their halting
  speech:

Humble lives to low thought, and low; but linked, to the
  thinker's eye,
By a bond that is stronger than death, with the lights of the
  farthest sky:

Here as there, the great drama of life rolled on, and a
  jubilant voice
Thrilled through me ineffable, vast, and bade me exult and
  rejoice "—

—rejoice in the knowledge of the goodness of
God. In the Creator as thus conceived of, we
have an object that calls for love, for admiration,

for self-surrendering devotion,—in a word, for worship.

Some one writes to me to say it would have been better, or at any rate more comforting, if in these sermons I had represented God as our heavenly Father, rather than as simply goodness, which sounds so cold and distant and unattractive. If it sounds so, this must be because we do not realise the full meaning of the word. Everything that is implied in the conception of the Divine Fatherhood, is implied in the conception of the Divine Goodness,—and more. All that is most lovable, all that is most adorable, is involved in the true conception of infinite goodness. And this conception, let me once more repeat, is an evolution from that of ordinary, finite, human goodness, with which men have been made acquainted in the ordinary experience of life.

In conclusion, may I just point out that here we find the very meaning and purpose of human affections. As it has been with the race, so it has been, and ever will be, with each individual. "That is not first which is spiritual, but that which is natural, and afterwards that which is spiritual." This truth has been very seldom understood, and never sufficiently insisted upon. According to one of the old misrepresentations of Christianity, we used to be told that in order to love God we must cease to love men, that we were to rise to the divine love by crushing out the human, that affection for the infinite was incompatible with affection for the finite, and that the former could only begin when the latter had been altogether annihilated. In the words of the old-fashioned orthodox hymn—

> " O not to one created thing
> Shall our embrace be given,
> But all our joy shall be in God,
> For only God is heaven."

This doctrine received some plausible support from certain misunderstood passages in the New Testament, such as " If a man hate not his father and his mother, he cannot be my disciple." But at the same time it is a doctrine exactly the opposite of the truth. It is a survival from the older religions, from religions falsely so called, in which all the frailties of men—amongst others jealousy and greed—were supposed to be characteristics of the Deity. It is a survival that dies but slowly. You remember Tennyson's words—

> "Forgive what seemed my sin in me;
> . . . . .
> Forgive my grief for one removed."

Whatever it may *seem*, love for a human being is no sin. In reality we shall learn to love God, not by learning to love His creatures less, but by learning to love them more,—with a purer, truer, intenser love. This world would be a strange preparation for the next if it were otherwise.

I should advise you all to read the 'Gates Ajar.' The heroine of that little story, Mary Cabot, had just lost her only brother, Roy, who was everything, more than everything, in the world to her. Left in her lonely wretchedness she soliloquises: "I think it must be there never was another like Roy. Then we had lived together so long, we two alone, since father died, that he had grown to me heart of my heart and life of my life. It did not seem as if he could be taken and I be left. Besides, I suppose most young women of my age have their dreams, and a future, probable or possible, which makes the very incompleteness of life sweet, because of the symmetry which is waiting somewhere. But that was settled so long ago for me that it makes it very different. Roy was all there was. . . . Roy, away in that dreadful heaven, can·have no thought of me, cannot remember how I loved him. The singing and the worshipping must take up all his time. God wants it all. He is a jealous God. I am nothing any more to Roy." Then people come to comfort her with the orthodox platitudes; and an elder of the Church pays her a long visit, in which he tries to improve the occasion for her soul's good, insisting on the fact that her bereavement must be a divine dispensation, and that Roy has been taken away because she so loved him. For Roy's sake therefore she hates the God in whom she has been taught to believe. And she does well to hate Him. She will not worship a Being who has given her the capacity to love and then crushes her for loving. She is right. Such worship would be the foulest blasphemy. So far good. She has got rid of the old and false religion. But at present she knows nothing of the true. She is taught it, however, slowly but very surely, by her aunt, a Mrs Fordyce, who is in my judgment one of the sweetest characters in American fiction. From her Mary Cabot learns the lesson which I have been trying to impress upon you to-day,—the lesson, viz., of the evolution of religion from human love.

Happy are we if we learn it too. It is interesting of course as a matter of philosophical theory; but it is even more important in its bearing on practical life. To try and crush the human affections, is not to develop, but to destroy, the divine. "If a man loveth not his brother whom he hath seen, how can he love God whom he hath not seen?" We cannot begin by loving the Infinite. If we ever love God at all, it will be, not by exterminating, but by cherishing and developing our love for the finite. "That is not first which is spiritual, but that which is natural; and afterwards that which is spiritual."

Little Kindnesses.

ONE of the best sermons I have read for a long time is to be found in last week's 'World.' It was called "Sins of Omission." The writer says: "The majority of us abstain from murder: we neither forge nor do we shoplift; and few of us have ever tried our hands at picking a pocket. For us the whole list of crimes and misdemeanours is fenced off and divided from our ordinary lives in the region of the impossible. With the exception of an occasional inclination to murder, which amidst the manifold provocations of daily life none of us can hope to escape, we can honestly declare that we have never been tempted. And yet we feel, most of us, that we are steeped in sin, and have fallen far away from the standard of an even philosophical Christianity,—ay, even from the gospel after Comte and George Eliot. Our lives are black with sins of omission—not the things we have done and ought not to have done, but the things we ought to have done and have not done. Frederica Bremer has touched this subject sweetly in one of her novels. A comfortable, motherly woman is driving home on Christmas Eve in a sledge, laden with cakes and toys and goodies for little people of her own; and at the turnpike the toll-keeper's children run out into the snow to look at her. She sees the humble interior in the fire-glow, and thinks she would like to give those little ones a few of her rosy apples and oranges and cakes; but the sledge drives on before she puts the thought into action. The sledge drives on, and the kindly act is left undone; the opportunity is lost. Life is full of such lost opportunities, full of the kindnesses we might have done, the people we might have helped, the tears we might have dried, the souls we might have saved perhaps,—putting the matter in its most serious aspect."

When I read this sermon in the 'World' I thought I would draw your attention to it, and perhaps add a few words of my own. Let me do so to-day. Let me speak to you for a moment or two about little kindnesses, — those little kindnesses which we all have it in our power to perform, but which for the most part we altogether omit.

It is strange that we human beings, who are ourselves such tiny specks in the infinite universe, should ignore and neglect what we are pleased to call "little things." We have such curious notions, too, as to the comparative greatness and littleness of things. The most important elements in our life are those which we, generally speaking, regard as trifles. They are the most important because they are always recurring. A farthing a minute is a great deal more than a pound a year. Our existence is made up of little things. Great joys, or what would commonly be called such, great successes, great opportunities for heroism, come but seldom, and in some lives never come at all. But little joys, little successes, little opportunities, may and do occur every hour, almost every moment of the day. If we neglect them, we shall be miserable when we might have been happy, we shall be nobodies when we might have been great.

> "This low man, adding one to one, his hundreds soon hit;
> That high man, aiming at a million, misses an unit."

So it is, too, with little kindnesses. We imagine it doesn't matter whether we confer them or not. But it does matter a great deal. I do not know of anything that matters more. Just let us consider what is lost by our neglecting them—lost in the life of the family, in the life of society, in the life of the community. A very little reflection upon this subject may help us to see how right Wordsworth was when he said, that the best portion of a good man's life consisted in

> "His little, nameless, unremembered acts
> Of kindness and of love."

What a different thing home-life would be if every member of every family were constantly doing little kindnesses to every other member. "Family jars" is a proverbial expression. To live with people, to be related to them, means very often to be made miserable by them. Some persons seem to imagine that their relations exist for the express purpose of being worried. And even in less extreme cases, even in cases where there is no very poignant misery in the family circle,—just think what an enormous amount of happiness there might be over and above what there actually is, if every member of the family always did his best to promote it. Some people are perfectly satisfied with themselves if they refrain from doing positive harm. They think themselves extremely amiable, if they are not aggressively unamiable. A man, for example, sometimes prides himself on being a good husband, because he does not beat his wife, does not very often snub her, and sometimes lets her have her own way. But as for trying to make her and keep her continuously happy,—well, he has got something else to think about. And this constant neglect of little happinesses leads in the long-run to great misery.

Read Carlyle's Diary. His wife was brilliant,[1] devoted, a woman of women; he accepted all her homage, all her faithful service, even to scrubbing floors and hunting noxious insects; and he

[1] I quote again from the writer in the 'World.'

neglected her. He allowed her to be dependent upon outside friendship, upon Darwin, upon Mill, for a drive or an ice; the modest luxury of a summer afternoon in the Park, and an ice at Gunter's—little pleasures which he could have given her so easily, and did not. The brougham which would have saved her long months of agony — the result of a fall while trying to scramble into an omnibus — the husband provided too late. All his sins against her were sins of omission—the sins of a man absorbed in his own work, thinking more of Frederick and his dry-as-dust German biographers than of the faithful, long-suffering wife. Never did he do her conscious or deliberate wrong; and he seemingly let her follow the bent of her own mind in cleaning rooms and riding in omnibuses. The sin was in not insisting upon better things; not perceiving that this bright creature was wasting health, talent, life, for his sake; not exercising an affectionate tyranny against those small economies, the scraping and paring that were no longer needful. And so, when she has gone from him, there goes up that bitter cry : "O, for five minutes more of her, to tell her with what love and admiration, as of the beautifullest of known human souls, I did intrinsically always regard her! . . . Thou who wouldst give, give quickly. In the grave thy loved one can receive no kindness. . . . Be wise, all ye living, and remember that time passes and does not return." I wonder whether there is any man present this morning who is treating his wife *à la* Carlyle.

And not only in the relations between husband and wife, but also in those between parents and children, between masters and servants, how much happiness is lost by the omission of little kindnesses! You have heard, I daresay, a good many sermons on the duties of children to their parents. Very comforting, no doubt, you found them. I am going to preach one some day on the duties of parents to their children. The latter set of duties are at least as numerous and as important as the former. Some people think they have done quite enough when they have fed and clothed and educated their children. They are satisfied, that is to say, when they have performed the duties for the neglect of which they could be punished by law. But moral duties and legal duties never altogether coincide. The scope of the former is always much more comprehensive than that of the latter. You have not fulfilled your duty to your children unless you have tried to secure for them all possible comfort and merriment and joy. And this you cannot do unless you are actuated by a spirit of continual kindliness. Whether your children are to be pitied or envied will depend, not so much upon their receiving, or failing to receive, occasional presents and treats, as upon their receiving, or failing to receive, small but ever-recurring kindnesses.

In regard to servants, again, masters and mistresses very often forget that duty is not all on the servants' side. Some people treat their dependents like machines—scrubbing-machines, cooking-machines, waiting-machines. And even if we are not quite so inhuman to our servants, few, if any of us, remember in regard to them the duty of little kindnesses—little kindnesses which might, and would, do a great deal to brighten lives that in the nature of things must be somewhat hard and dull.

I need not say much about little kindnesses in

society. To some extent we are forced to them, or at any rate to the semblance of them, by etiquette, fashion and good manners. A man would lose caste—would, in fact, be excommunicated—if he were guilty in society of rudenesses, which he may commit with impunity when he is in the bosom of his family. It is sad but true that home is the place in which an immense number of men appear at their worst. But though a certain amount of decent courtesy is *required* of you in society, you must go beyond what is absolutely necessary, if you wish to do your social duty—nay, even if you wish to be considered agreeable. A kindly heart will help you very much with your manners. The manners of a perfect Christian would not differ in essential respects from the manners of a perfect courtier. Nay, more, without kindliness no one can be quite a gentleman. The Prince of Wales is a great example to us in this respect. I have often seen him talk to an old lady, or even to an old gentleman, with as much courtesy and consideration and charm as if he had been in the presence of a reigning beauty. Why cannot we always remember that we have a duty to perform towards those whom we meet in society,—the ladies, for example, whom we take down to dinner, the girls with whom we dance, the people who are staying with us in a country house? If we were always actuated by the spirit of kindliness, they would all be the happier for meeting us, they would all be thankful that they knew us.

Then there is the duty of little kindnesses to the poor. I don't mean giving money to beggars. That is the only little kindness which some people ever indulge in; but such little kindnesses are in reality great unkindnesses. Beggars, in ninety-nine cases out of a hundred, are rascals. Giving them money therefore is the encouragement of rascality, which can neither be for the good of the community nor for that of the individual who is so encouraged. The same remark applies to General Booth's silly and highly reprehensible project of giving dinners, at less than cost price, to all the lazy loafers who may condescend to accept them. The General must either be ignorant of the first principles of political economy, or else he must be willing to swell the numbers of his army at no matter what sacrifice to the State. His plan would tend directly to the multiplication of paupers and idlers. If you have any money to give away, and are really actuated by the spirit of kindliness, you will take the trouble to inquire into the merits of the recipients. Should that be too much exertion for you, you will at any rate give your money to the Charity Organisation Society, or some such institution, which will undertake to see that it is not misspent. If you want to do any good in the world, it is not enough to have a kindly heart, you must have also a wise head and some common-sense. You must think a little. I am sorry—but you must. And if your kindliness of heart will not induce you to take this much trouble, I don't attach much value to it. It must be a very feeble kindliness,—rather a silly sentimentalism than real goodness.

And there are many other little kindnesses we can show the poor besides giving them money—kindnesses the importance of which it is impossible to overrate. Here, again, there is much to be done by manner. A genial smile, a gentle tone, a hearty shake of the hand,—simple things like these will often do much good, and the omission of them much harm. What a difference there is in the way in which people shake hands, and what a different effect they produce on us! Some do it in a way which says plainly enough, "What a bore it is to have to go through this silly ceremony!" And others do it as if they enjoyed it, as if they meant it, as if they were really glad to see us. In the one case we feel chilled and uncomfortable. In the other we go away feeling on good terms with ourselves and everybody else; life suddenly appears to us richer and brighter than it did a moment before.

Let me entreat you then, in conclusion, to ponder seriously over the value — the infinite value — of little kindnesses. Life is made up of little events. Happiness is made up of little pleasures. We are all able to confer innumerable little kindnesses on our family, on our servants, on our acquaintances. Each of us may do thousands, millions, billions of them. You have only to add them together, in order to see that they form by far the most important part of human conduct.

> "O the little more, and how much it is!
> O the little less, and what worlds away!"

Laughter.

"When the Lord turned again the captivity of Zion . . . our mouth was filled with laughter."—Ps. cxxvi. 1, 2.

LAUGHTER represented as the gift of God to His chosen people! Yet the English puritan shrinks from it as if it were unholy and profane. I recently received the following letter:—

"Common Room,
Lincoln's Inn, *January* 22.

"Dear Sir,—Last Sunday morning I went to the Foundling and heard you preach. In the midst of your sermon there was a positive outbreak of laughter, stifled, I admit, but nevertheless distinctly audible all over the Church. This unseemly exhibition you permitted to pass unnoticed. I make no comment, but leave you to consider in what way this reflects upon the clergy of our Church.—I am, Sir, yours faithfully,   HENRY ST JOHN DAWSON."

Mr Dawson is a type of many religious or professedly religious persons. He shudders if a laugh occurs during the sermon, as a Jew might have shuddered had he seen the devil sitting in the holy of holies. I do not suppose Mr Dawson would object to the congregation crying. Tears he would consider pious; laughter, at any rate in connection with serious subjects, he considers impious. I have written to tell him that I shall read his letter to you this morning, as it will serve to illustrate a doctrine which I consider false and pernicious.

I do not propose to-day to discuss the subject of preaching.[1] I am not going to inquire how far the sense of humour should be appealed to from the pulpit. But let me make one remark in passing. If the sermon is worthy of the name —I need hardly say most sermons are not—but if it is, it is a work of art. There is an art of

[1] On that see my 'Preaching and Hearing.'

words, no less than an art of colours. Now humour and pathos are in speech what lights and shades are in painting, and the highest artist is he who succeeds in combining them most skilfully. The preacher who is in earnest, who is determined to secure the attention and the interest of his hearers, who is eager to convince and to persuade them, will appeal to all their faculties, the sense of humour among the number, if he can. If he can! For some people do not possess this most valuable gift. And I was shocked to read the other day in the 'Irish Ecclesiastical Gazette' that I was to be reckoned amongst that most unhappy number. In a kindly and complimentary review of my last book, the critic said that my sermons reminded him of those of a celebrated church dignitary, *minus* the sense of humour. "For Professor Momerie has no humour. He is awfully in earnest. His style is dry, we would almost say acrid." If that reviewer is right, I am sorry—sorry for myself, and still sorrier for you. Humour is the most persuasive of all the expedients which an orator can command. And if preaching is anything but a farce, if it means anything, if it is ever to accomplish anything, the preacher's sense of humour must be considered as pre-eminently a gift of God. *Pre-eminently.*

However, I do not want to speak to-day particularly of sermons. I rather want to draw your attention to the general doctrine which is so common amongst us, that merriment is incompatible with seriousness, that dulness and melancholy are the peculiar signs of religion.

I admit of course, it is scarcely necessary to say, that there are occasions in life when laughter would be out of place, and therefore unseemly. But the same is true of tears. Tears may sometimes be an insult. Tears are occasionally the signs of madness. I admit of course, it is scarcely necessary to say, that laughter may sometimes be silly, that merriment may sometimes be profane. There is a laughter, there is a merriment, unworthy of the name, just as there is poisonous food and adulterated wine. The true merriment may be distinguished from the false by the fact that it bears reflection; we can think of it with pleasure next day and next week. It is a joy for ever. The doctrine I wish to condemn is the doctrine that *all* merriment, even the best, is worthless, or comparatively worthless; that laughter is *always* inferior to tears; that, as Lewis Morris puts it,

"Tears are divine, but mirth is of the earth."

I say it is a false doctrine, and like all false doctrines mischievous. It is a gratuitous assumption, for which there is not a particle of evidence. There is overwhelming evidence against it. Tears mean that something is wrong with us; laughter means that we are happy. Surely, if you come to think of it, you will see it is nothing short of blasphemy to assert that the only gift we receive from God is wretchedness. Moreover, tears are but a temporary accident, attending the earlier and imperfect stages of evolution. There will come a time, the Bible tells us, when there shall be no more tears. That is never said of laughter. Again, laughter is one of the criteria of goodness. A villain never laughs. What Shakespeare said of music is just as true of laughter—

> "The man that hath no laughter in himself
> Is fit for treasons, stratagems, and spoils.
> The motions of his spirit are dull as night,
> And his affections dark as Erebus.
> Let no such man be trusted."

On the other hand, as Carlyle says, "no one who has once heartily laughed can be irreclaimably bad." You may always trust the man whose laughter has a genuine ring about it. These facts alone would suffice to show that laughter cannot be an evil, not even a silly, thing.

Further and specially, laughter, merriment, cheerfulness, and everything that conduces to cheerfulness, are absolutely essential to enable us to live our best. Life is so serious, you may say, that the man who is in earnest will have no time for laughter. I tell you, it is just because life is so serious, that we need all the laughter we can get to help us through with it. You may think too much of the seriousness of life. You may brood over the tragic side of human experience till you find yourself in a madhouse.[1] And what

---

[1] "Wir menschen werden wunderbar geprüft;
Wir könnten's nicht ertragen, hätt' uns nicht
Denholden Leichtsinn die Natur verliehn."
—*Torquato Tasso*, ii. 4.

would be the good of that? A man's first business, say the Puritans, is to battle with his temptations, and with these temptations, therefore, his thoughts should be entirely engrossed. I tell you he will best battle with his temptations by drawing his thoughts away from them. And here laughter and merriment, no less than healthy occupation, have their part to play. Cheerful amusements have saved many a soul from death.

Mr Louis Stevenson spoke very wisely on this point in an article which appeared lately in 'Scribner,' entitled "A Christmas Sermon." "A man may have a flaw, a weakness, that unfits him for the duties of life, that spoils his temper, that threatens his integrity, or that betrays him into cruelty. It has to be conquered; but it must never be suffered to engross his thoughts. The true duties lie all upon the farther side, and must be attended to with a whole mind, as soon as this preliminary clearing of the decks has been effected. In order that he may be kind and honest, it may be needful he should become a total abstainer; let him become so then,—and the next day let him forget the circumstance. A mortified appetite is never a wise companion."

And not only in regard to temptation, but in regard to our daily business, laughter and merriment will be of the greatest possible assistance. You all know, I suppose, the bad effects of worry, anxiety, and despondency; how they upset the digestion, derange the liver, and incapacitate a man for work. Well, cheerfulness has just the opposite effect. It has more to do with our health than either food or drink. It "doeth good like a medicine." It is the best of tonics. Of all silly delusions, perhaps the silliest is the notion that time given up to amusements is wasted time. It is no more wasted than meal-time or bed-time. Most truly are amusements called recreations, for we are re-created by them. You see then, do you not, the importance of cultivating cheerfulness and everything that conduces to cheerfulness, if you would do your duty towards yourselves?

And it is even more important, if possible, that you should cultivate cheerfulness, if you would fulfil your duty towards your neighbours. It is your duty to do all that in you lies to make your neighbours happy. But if you are of a gloomy and morose disposition, if you look askance at merriment and laughter, you will do all that in you lies to make them wretched. "A strange temptation," says Mr Louis Stevenson in the sermon from which I have already quoted,—" a strange temptation attends upon man to keep his eye on pleasures, even when he will not share in them. At any excess or perversion of a natural appetite the lyre of certain moralists sounds of itself with relishing denunciations; but for all displays of the truly diabolic—envy, malice, the mean lie, the mean silence, the calumnious truth, the backbiter, the petty tyrant, the peevish poisoner of family life—their standard is quite different. These are wrong, they will admit, yet somehow not so wrong; there is no zeal in their assaults upon them; no secret element of gusto warms the sermon: it is for things not wrong in themselves that they reserve the choicest of their indignation. . . . In each of us some similar tendency resides. The sight of a pleasure, in which we cannot or will not share, moves us to a particular impatience. It may be because we are envious, or because we are sad, or because we dislike noise and romping—being so refined, or because, being so philosophic, we have an overwhelming sense of life's gravity; but at least as we go on in years we are all of us tempted to frown upon our neighbour's pleasures. People are fond nowadays of resisting temptation; here is one to be resisted. They are fond of self-denial; here is one that cannot be too peremptorily inculcated. There is an idea abroad among moral people that they should make their neighbours good. One person I have to make good—myself. But my duty to my neighbour is much more nearly expressed by saying that I have to make him happy—if I may.[1] . . . The kingdom of heaven is of the childlike, of those who are easy to please, who love and give pleasure. Gentleness and cheerfulness, —these come before all morality; they are the perfect duties. And it is the trouble with moral men that they have neither the one nor the other. It was the moral man, the Pharisee, whom Christ could not away with. If your morals make you

[1] The philosophical reader will remember the same doctrine in Kant's Ethics.

dreary, depend upon it they are wrong. I do not say 'Give them up,' for they may be all you have; but conceal them like a vice, lest they should spoil the lives of better men than yourselves."

Now I am afraid that this tendency to moroseness is the Englishman's besetting sin. There are cheerful, genial, merry men and women amongst us, thank God! but probably the *proportion* of morose men and women is greater than in any other country in the world. This is due in great measure to our detestable climate. Unless one has a cast-iron constitution, it is not easy to be cheerful in a fog; it is difficult not to be morose. All the more necessary therefore that we should be on our guard. It is the sin which doth so easily and constantly beset us that we must of all others endeavour to lay aside. M. Taine, in his 'History of English Literature,' has some amusing remarks on the influence of our climate upon our character. He shows how it has tended to make us sombre, heavy, sad, hateful. Pleasure was out of the question, he says, in such an atmosphere, and therefore we gave ourselves up to morality,—the unlovable morality of Puritanism. But, believe me, this morality—in so far as it is unlovable, in so far as it makes us melancholy in ourselves and morose to others—is not real morality. Genuine morality is not gloomy; it is lovable and gay. A man who keeps about three of the commandments expects to be called a moral man. What nonsense! Such a man may be, and often is, in spite of his three "virtues," a curse to all who know him. Without laughter, without merriment, without perpetual cheerfulness, we shall never make the best of ourselves, we shall never do our best in the world. If we care for ourselves therefore, if we care for others, we shall do everything in our power to cultivate a gladsome, merry disposition. "A merry heart doth good like a medicine." And yet so few Englishmen possess it. As a nation we have long been kept under the hateful yoke of Puritanism. But we are not to remain under it for ever. We are already struggling to shake it off. And when at last we are free from this accursed bondage, when the Lord turns again our captivity, our mouths will be filled with laughter.

The Resurrection of the Body.

SOME time ago, after I had been preaching upon Immortality, I received the following anonymous letter:—

"SIR,—From what you said yesterday, I gather that you do not believe in the Resurrection of the Body. But if there is no resurrection, how shall I be able to recognise my friends in the next life? To console myself, when I got home I read the 15th chapter of the 1st Epistle to the Corinthians."

Now I am always grateful for such foolish letters. I will tell you why. One of the chief difficulties which a public teacher has to contend with is this. The persons who hold the errors and superstitions which he attacks, constantly accuse him of having misrepresented them. It is eminently satisfactory therefore to possess in black and white the statement of their views from one of themselves. My anonymous friend represents a very large class. He believes in the resurrection of the body, using the word body in its ordinary sense. He does not see that such a belief is repugnant to common-sense, that it involves the grossest absurdities, and that the profession of it as an article of faith is most dishonouring to the Deity.

To begin with, I must point out the impropriety of speaking of the resurrection of *the* body, as if you had only one! The substance of your physical organism is constantly changing. You have to-day an entirely different body from that which you had a few years ago, and from that which you will have a few years hence. Which of these bodies is to rise again? It has occasionally been held that they are all to be raised; that every particle of matter, which ever formed part of an individual's organism upon earth, will be incorporated into his resurrection body. At that rate you would begin the next life weighing many tons,—an unwieldy condition, forsooth, in which to enter into the spiritual world.

More generally, however, it has been held that the body to be raised is the body deposited in the grave. But this view involves just as much absurdity as the other. Every one knows that the buried body soon mingles with the surrounding elements, and therefore *as a body* it ceases to exist. It is said God could miraculously call together the scattered particles, and cause them to reconstitute the old organism. Whether God could do so or not, we need not trouble to inquire. We may be very sure that He would not. For consider: the body which is consigned to the grave is the body which has been wasted by disease or mutilated by accident. What an inheritance with which to start in another world! I heard recently of a man whose leg had been amputated and put in a glass case for purposes of medical study. He afterwards removed to a distant parish, but gave orders in his will that he was to be buried in the same parish with his leg,—in order that he might conveniently find it at the resurrection. Even supposing he did find it; even supposing there was some angelic surgeon, capable of reuniting him with his long-lost member and removing from that member the disease for which it was originally cut off, it would never be quite as good a leg as the other. A mended limb, however skilfully the surgical operation may be performed, is always liable at any rate—to be affected by changes in the weather. Again, if the popular theory were true, there would often be rival claimants for the same body. When a cannibal eats a missionary, the organism of the latter becomes part of the organism of the former. In the resurrection therefore, according to the common view, there would only be one body between them. You may say the body belonged by rights to the missionary, and that it would therefore be restored to him. But however just this proceeding might be, the cannibal would be left without any body at all, and consequently the popular theory of the resurrection would not in his case hold good. And even if we live to a good old age, and die placidly without accident, without any perceptible disease, still the body which our friends will bury is not the body at its best, but at its worst,—feeble, wasted, worn out, dead. If we really believed in the resurrection of the body we should pray above all things to die in our prime. To live to old age, and to have the old body raised again, would mean a future life of eternal weakness and decrepitude. As for recognition in the future, the resurrection of the body would frequently render it impossible. Some time ago I was calling on a young lady who had just lost her husband. She said—"It has changed me so, that if he were to see me now, even after these few days, he would scarcely know me." Hard on her, hard on him, if she, whom he left young and beautiful, is to meet him in the next life an old, haggard, worn-out woman!

Some persons, who have perceived the difficulties that beset the popular view, and who still wish to believe in the resurrection of the body, have maintained that a new body is to be formed, not containing the old particles of matter, but merely composed of the same chemical elements—carbon, hydrogen, nitrogen, oxygen, with a dash of phosphorus and iron. Now this theory at first sight is less ludicrous than the others. But if you think for a moment, you will see that it involves at least one fatal absurdity. It provides us, or rather encumbers us, with a material body, when we are about to enter into a spiritual world. Common-sense—called common ironically, I suppose, because it is the rarest of all senses—common-sense tells us that such a theory of the resurrection is a contradiction in terms, and therefore an impossibility. And not only is the theory in itself inherently ridiculous—it is most distinctly denied and repudiated in the Bible. "Flesh and blood," says St Paul, "cannot enter into the kingdom of God." So that if a material body were given to any one after death, he would be thereby prevented, then as now, from entering into the spiritual realm.

It often happens—and this is especially, remarkably, apparent in regard to the resurrection—that the Bible is so much wiser, so much more rational, than the orthodox allow. I have called your attention to this subject because it seems to me that a grievous injury is done to Christianity and to Christ, by the crude and silly ideas regarding the resurrection, which are frequently held and professed by persons who call themselves Christians. It would be bad enough to hold the doctrines, but to assert that they are the doctrines of the Bible is to pour shame and contempt upon that sacred book. There is nothing which is more fatal to the progress of religion, there is nothing which gives more frequent occasion to the enemies of Christianity to blaspheme, than stupidity. And of all forms of theological stupidity, the most aggravating, the most inexcusable, and the most pernicious, is that which persists in finding in the Bible what is not there, which persists in maintaining that the Bible teaches what it plainly and unmistakably denies. There are many bibliolators — that is to say, worshippers of the Bible, people who profess to believe in its absolute infallibility—whose theological ideas nevertheless are quite out of harmony with, very often in flagrant contradiction to, Biblical teaching. Where these ideas come from, I do not know. But having got them, they seem to argue naïvely thus—such an excellent book as the Bible is bound to support the views of such excellent people as ourselves. My anonymous friend, for example, my foolish anonymous friend, who had made up his mind that there was to be a resurrection of the body, after listening to my sermon which somewhat disconcerted him, went home and consoled himself "by reading the fifteenth chapter of the 1st Epistle to the Corinthians." It hardly seems credible! But the gentleman gives us his word for it. He wanted his faith in the resurrection of the body confirmed, and he got it confirmed by reading a chapter which asserts the very contrary. "Thou sowest *not* that body which shall be." It is impossible for human language to be plainer. Look at the context. "Some will say, How are the dead raised up? and with what body do they come? Fool! Thou sowest not that body that shall be. It is sown in corruption, it is raised in incorruption; it is sown in dishonour, it is raised in glory; it is sown in weakness, it is raised in power; it is sown a natural body, it is raised a spiritual body." The resurrection-body then, the body with which we are to enter into another life, is not the worn-out organism of the flesh; it is not a chemical combination of carbon, hydrogen, nitrogen, and oxygen, with a dash of phosphorus and iron. Such a body at the best is material, and its characteristics must always be corruption, weakness, and consequent dishonour. The resurrection-body is a spiritual body, and its attributes are incorruption, power, glory.

The fifteenth chapter of the 1st Epistle to the Corinthians is not the only place in the Bible where this spiritual doctrine of the resurrection is taught. The same idea occurred to Job[1] in a moment of prophetic inspiration. But it attracted very little attention for centuries after that book was written; and unfortunately the passage is so mistranslated in our Authorised Version, that its real meaning is quite lost for the English reader. Job is firmly persuaded that his friends have accused him wrongfully; he is fully convinced that sooner or later—in the far-off future if not in the present, in the next world if not in this—the Almighty will declare him innocent. "I know,"

[1] Job xix. 25.

he says, "that my Avenger liveth, and that he will stand at last over my dust; that, after my body has been destroyed, without my flesh I shall see God." A Hebrew would understand by the avenger the nearest relative of the deceased, whose business it was to take cognisance of any wrongs that had been done to his departed kinsman. Job's idea in this passage is that there will come a time when God, who seems now to have forsaken him, will act the part of this avenging friend,—that the Almighty will one day stand solemnly over his grave and conclusively vindicate his character. And Job further believed he himself would then be alive; that though his flesh would have seen corruption, with the eyes of a spiritual body he would behold his divine Avenger.

In conclusion, I should like to point out to you that the spiritual body, though spiritual, is a body nevertheless,—an organism fitted to be the instrument of the mind.

"Eternal form will still divide
The eternal soul from all beside."

We have not, of course—we cannot expect to have at present—any definite knowledge regarding the spiritual body. Spiritual things are spiritually discerned; a spiritual body cannot be cognised through material organs. The best speculations on the subject hitherto have been those of Swedenborg; but I would remind you they are *only* speculations. If you will bear this in mind, there is a little book which you may read with interest and profit. It is called 'The Nature of Spirit,' and is written by the Rev. Chauncey Giles. It gives a popular account of Swedenborg's views. Personally, if you care to know, I think it possible, probable, that the spiritual body may bear a close resemblance to the physical—such a close resemblance perhaps as is borne, or supposed to be borne, by the astral body and by the wraith. It is curious to notice in the Gospels the twofold assertion, that Christ's body was recognised by His disciples after the resurrection, and yet that it was capable of passing silently and easily through closed doors and windows. But how far the analogy may hold good between the physical and the spiritual body, how far they may resemble one another, I do not know; nor does any one else. We may well believe that the resurrection-body is not subject to the imperfections and limitations of matter, and that therefore it is a far more effective instrument for the mind than the present physical organism. Whether the resurrection-body is now in existence, or whether it has yet to be created, I do not know; nor does any one else.[1] Personally, I think it probable that death and resurrection are identical; that the dissolution of the physical body leads directly and immediately to the birth of the spiritual body; in other words, that death introduces the spirit into a spiritual environment where the spiritual organism can work.

But speculation apart, if we listen to the teaching of common-sense, if we listen to the teaching of the Bible, we shall learn once and for ever to disbelieve in the physical theory of the resurrection. And that is most important. People talk a great deal about the necessity for belief. I wish they would talk sometimes about the necessity for disbelief. Giving up

---

[1] There are some interesting speculations on this subject in the 'Unseen Universe.'

error is the first step towards reaching truth. The old vulgar theory of the resurrection made the universe appear contemptible,—made the Deity Himself an object for our scorn. A physical resurrection would stultify the whole course of evolution. What God is going to do with us, we do not know. Eye hath not seen, ear hath not heard, neither hath it entered, neither can it enter, into the heart of man to conceive the things which God hath prepared. But if we know—as know we may—that He will certainly do nothing unworthy of Himself or of us, then we can die, as we have lived, in full assurance of faith. With our last expiring breath we can say calmly, hopefully, triumphantly—

> "To Him I yield my spirit,
> On Him I lay my load;
> Fear ends with death: beyond it
> I nothing see but God."

The Gods of the Bible.

" I the Lord thy God am a jealous God, visiting the iniquity of the fathers upon the children unto the third and fourth generation of them that hate me; and showing mercy unto thousands of them that love me."—Ex. xx. 5, 6.

" If ye love them that love you, what thank have ye? for sinners also love those that love them. And if ye do good to them which do good to you, what thank have ye? for sinners also do even the same. And if ye lend to them of whom ye hope to receive, what thank have ye? for sinners also lend to sinners, hoping to receive as much again. But love ye your enemies, and do good, and lend, hoping for nothing again; and your reward shall be great, and ye shall be the children of the Highest: for He is kind unto the unthankful and the evil."—LUKE vi. 32-35.

SOME people think the Bible is a single book. If you asked them *why*, they would be rather puzzled. They might perhaps say, because it is bound by a single cover. I cannot think of any other reason. With the exception of the cover, everything connected with the Bible tends to show that it is a collection of many books, written by very different men with very different ideas and motives. The opinions which the writers hold upon moral and religious subjects are frequently opposed and contradictory. Let me repeat what I said when I preached upon the subject of Inspiration. We cannot possibly over-estimate the difference—it is practically infinite—between the God of Samuel who ordered infants and sucklings to be slaughtered, and the God of the Psalmist whose tender mercies are over all His works; between the God of the patriarchs who was always repenting, and the God of the apostles who is the same yesterday, to-day and for ever, with whom there is neither variableness nor shadow of turning; between the God of the Old Testament who walked in the garden in the cool of the day, and the God of the New Testament whom no man hath seen nor can see; between the God of Leviticus who was so particular about the sacrificial furniture and utensils, and the God of the Acts who dwelleth not in temples made with hands; between the God who hardened Pharaoh's heart, and the God who will have all men to be saved. We find in the Bible theological opinions as diverse and contradictory as have ever existed in the world.

The passages which I read just now as a text afford an interesting illustration of this extreme discrepancy. The conduct which in the first passage is said to be characteristic of the Deity is in the second passage attributed to sinners. According to the author of the twentieth chapter of the Book of Exodus, God is merciful only to those who love Him. According to Christ, that would be a poor kind of mercy; the true God, the Heavenly Father, is kind unto the unthankful and the evil. It seems scarcely credible that for centuries men should have read these passages without seeing their discrepancy, without seeing that they represented different stages in the evolution of the idea of God. Even now the very suggestion of such discrepancy would by many persons be considered heresy. But—heresy or not—the discrepancy is palpable, self-evident, undeniable, for all who will attend to the meaning of words. The mischief is, people will not attend to the meaning of words. They are the slaves of a foregone conclusion. They have made up their minds that the Bible is one book, not many; and they proceed to interpret, or rather misinterpret, everything in the Bible, so as to harmonise with their false and foolish hypothesis.

I know it may be said that—Christ notwithstanding—what the second commandment tells us about the visitation of iniquity to the third and fourth generation is true. I do not deny it; it is true. It is but the scientific doctrine of heredity. And in fact we should now state the truth much more strongly. The consequences of iniquity descend from the fathers to the children far beyond the third and fourth generations. They will be transmitted to the end of time. *But there is an heredity of goodness as well as an heredity of evil; and in the second commandment this is altogether ignored.* Further, the very heredity of evil is not, as seems to be implied in Exodus, vindictive and retaliative. It is, after all, a merciful law; for there is no greater stimulus to right-doing than the clear recognition of the fact that our descendants will suffer for our sins. The writer in Exodus gives, you see, only a one-sided statement of the doctrine of heredity, and so he practically represents the Deity as acting in a way which Christ most emphatically condemned. "Ye have heard that it hath been said, Thou shalt love thy neighbour, and hate thine enemy. But I say unto you, Love your enemies, bless them that curse you, do good to them that hate you, and pray for them which despitefully use you and persecute you; that ye may be the children of your Father which is in heaven : for He maketh His sun to rise on the evil and on the good, and sendeth rain on the just and on the unjust. But if ye love them which love you, what reward have ye? do not even the publicans the same?" [The publicans were the collectors of the Roman taxes, and were probably very often extortionate and unjust. But in any case they were hated, because they represented a foreign yoke. The tax-gatherers were regarded by the Jews as the meanest and lowest class of humanity.] "And if ye salute your brethren only, what do ye more than others? do not even the tax-gatherers so? Be ye therefore perfect, even as your Father which is in heaven is perfect." God shows mercy not only, as the second commandment tell us, to those who love Him, but even, says Christ, to those who hate Him. And the law of heredity is no exception to His mercy, but the outcome of it.

Let me read you part of a brilliant letter I received upon this subject some time ago. "Is it wonderful, when two such widely different standards of morality are set before us as equally final and equally authoritative, that the larger number of so-called Christians should choose the lower and easier of attainment, and that we should so often hear it said almost complacently, 'Oh! when people behave well to me, I am always a good friend to them; but if once they deceive me, I have done with them? I never forget.'" Such words are flagrantly unchristian, and yet they exactly express the sentiments of the Jewish Jehovah.

"And further," continues my correspondent, "is not the second commandment answerable for the horrible doctrine which still tortures the hearts of many, that we must be careful not to love any one too much for fear we should come to love him more than God? I know I was always taught to draw this lesson from it. And though no doubt the idea would not be forced so explicitly on children brought up less Calvinistically, still implicitly it has been widespread in its influence, and has perhaps done more than anything else to alienate loving hearts from God. Mothers have feared to love their children too well, lest 'the jealous God' should take them away; and have had to try and teach their children to be cool in their affection, lest God in His anger should leave them motherless. Has not every one heard some despairing cry like Mary Cabot's,[1] after the death of her brother—'God wants all his love. He is a jealous God. I am nothing any more to Roy.' Only last summer I heard a sermon in a Presbyterian church in Ireland, upon Agag and his people; and in this sermon the preacher insisted that the god who commanded their wholesale destruction is the same yesterday, to-day and for ever. Is it not time that we left off applying the worst characteristics of the Jewish Jehovah to the heavenly Father of Christ?"

I answer, yes it is, high time! It should re-

[1] See pp. 193, 194.

quire but a very little reflection to see that the superhuman cruelty of the Jehovah of the Pentateuch, and the superhuman tenderness of the Father of Christ, are contradictory attributes, which cannot possibly belong to one and the self-same Being. If the books that make up our Bible had been bound separately instead of together, deities so essentially different would never have been confounded. But manifestly two different Beings are not converted into one, because they both happen to be described within the covers of a single volume. Words like those of the second commandment, if found in the sacred literature of a pagan tribe, would be used by Christian apologists for the purpose of showing that Christianity was superior to paganism: and they serve equally well to show that Christianity is superior to Judaism—especially to Judaism at its worst.

I say to Judaism at its worst, because Judaism had a better side. There is a great deal of evolution within the limits of the Old Testament itself. In the words of some of the Psalmists and of some of the prophets, we find foreshadowings of the teaching of Christ. There is evolution often within the limits of the same book. In this very book of Exodus, for example, the Deity in one place is described as "forgiving iniquity and transgression." But I am speaking to-day exclusively of the view which is taken in the second commandment; and here we have Judaism at its lowest level. Jehovah is represented as merely one amongst a number of competing Deities. He has somewhat more power than they, but He is not a whit less vindictive or cruel. He visits the sins of the fathers upon the children unto the third and fourth generation of those that hate Him; and shows mercy only to those that love Him. I know of nothing in the world more thoroughly alien to the spirit of Christianity.

I want you to think carefully over what I have said. In the past men have cared more for the infallibility of their Bible than for the morality of their God. And unless before very long there be a change in this respect, I fear that religion will be swept from off the face of the earth. "The reason," says Hawthorne, "why the mass of men fear God, and at bottom dislike Him, is because they distrust His heart." But a God whose heart can be distrusted is in reality no God; he is but an idol,—a false imagination of ignorant men. With the progress of knowledge this fact will become generally recognised. The only God who can permanently survive, the only God whom men will permanently worship, is the God of love. And if He too is degraded, the time is not far distant when He too will come to be regarded as merely the product of a diseased imagination. I adjure you, therefore, if you call yourselves Christians, if you think you believe in the God of Christ, be very careful that you do not confuse Him with inferior deities, with false gods. If you attribute to Him, if you allow to be attributed to Him, characteristics unworthy of a man; if you attribute to Him, if you allow to be attributed to Him, characteristics that are incompatible with infinite and eternal love,—you are worse enemies to the cause of real religion than the most virulent of open and professed atheists. Beware! The time is coming when judgment must first begin at the house of God.

I will read you in conclusion a poem of Whittier's, called "The Eternal Goodness."

The Gods of the Bible.

"O friends! with whom my feet have trod
    The quiet aisles of prayer,
Glad witness to your zeal for God
    And love of man I bear.

I trace your lines of argument;
    Your logic linked and strong
I weigh, as one who dreads dissent
    And fears a doubt as wrong.

But still my human hands are weak
    To hold your iron creeds:
Against the words ye bid me speak
    My heart within me pleads.

I walk with bare, hushed feet the ground
    Ye tread with boldness shod;
I dare not fix with mete and bound
    The loving power of God.

Ye praise His justice; even such
    His pitying love I deem:
Ye seek a king; I fain would touch
    The robe that hath no seam.

Ye see the curse which overbroods
    A world of pain and loss;
I hear our Lord's beatitudes,
    And prayer upon the cross.

More than your schoolmen teach, within
    Myself, alas! I know;
Too dark ye cannot paint the sin;
    Too small the merit show.

I bow my forehead to the dust,
    I veil mine eyes for shame,
And urge in trembling self-distrust
    A prayer without a claim.

I see the wrong that round me lies,
    I feel the guilt within;
I hear, with groan and travail-cries,
    The world confess its sin.

Yet in the maddening maze of things,
    And tossed by storm and flood,
To one fixed stake my spirit clings,—
    I know that God is good.

Not mine to look where cherubim
    And seraphs may not see,—
But nothing can be good in Him
    Which evil is in me.

The wrong that pains my soul below
    I dare not throne above:
I know not of His hate; I know
    His goodness and His love.

I dimly guess from blessings known
    Of greater out of sight,
And, with the chastened Psalmist, own
    His judgments too are right.

I know not what the future hath
    Of marvel or surprise;
Assured alone that life and death
    His mercy underlies.

And so beside the silent sea,
   I wait the muffled oar;
No harm from Him can come to me
   On ocean or on shore.

I know not where His islands lift
   Their fronded palms in air;
I only know I cannot drift
   Beyond His love and care.

Do thou, O Lord! by whom are seen
   Thy creatures as they be,
Forgive me, if too close I lean
   My human heart on Thee!"

The Didache; or, Teaching of the Twelve Apostles.

I HAVE explained to you[1] how the particular books which we now find in "the Bible" came to be there. This subject is generally shrouded in a great deal of unnecessary mystery. In reality there is no mystery about it. It might be, and should be, explained to Sunday-school children. Whatever theory of "inspiration" you may hold, you must remember that the books of Scripture were collected together by synods or councils, composed of men for whom no inspiration, in the orthodox sense of the word, can be claimed. Nor indeed can it be claimed for them in any sense. For they have frequently contradicted one another, and it is manifest that two contradictory statements

[1] See 'Inspiration,' pp. 76-88.

cannot both be inspired. The non-inspiration of councils is recognised by our Church in one of the Articles.[1] "General Councils, forasmuch as they be an assembly of men whereof all be not governed by the Spirit and Word of God, may, and sometimes have, erred." In fact, a council is only the ecclesiastical word for a committee. At committee meetings of rabbis in the case of the Old Testament, of bishops in the case of the New, it was determined whether a book should be admitted into the sacred canon or not.

I explained to you that several books, after being for a long time rejected, were finally received; as for example, the Song of Solomon, Ecclesiastes and Revelation. Some of the doubtful books, however, never got into the canon at all. And of these a little treatise called the 'Teaching of the Twelve Apostles' was one. This book was called scripture by a "father" of the Church, Clement of Alexandria, at the end of the first century.[2] Later on, Eusebius mentions it

---

[1] The twenty-first.
[2] "The scripture saith, Son, be not a liar, for lying leadeth to theft."—Strom. i. 20.

as one of the disputed books (*Anti-legomena*). But he includes the Apocalypse in the same category. Now, the reason why one of these disputed books was eventually taken, and the other left, was this. The Apocalypse was, or was supposed to be, written by an apostle, but the Teaching was not. And there was a strong determination to restrict the canon to apostolic writings. On this ground, however, the Epistle to the Hebrews should have been excluded. The early councils thought it was written by St Paul; but it was not, nor indeed by any apostle. It follows therefore that the 'Teaching of the Twelve Apostles' was *unfairly* excluded; for its non-apostolic authorship seems to have been the only argument against it.

But having been rejected it soon came to be ignored. It is mentioned by Athanasius in the fourth century, Anastasius in the sixth, Joannes Zouaras in the twelfth, and Matthæus Blastares in the fourteenth. After that the treatise seems to have been entirely forgotten until modern times. It was rediscovered in 1873 by Bryennios, Metropolitan of Nicomedia in Asia Minor.

He found a MS. copy of it in the library attached to the monastery of the most Holy Sepulchre in Constantinople. This MS. was written in 1056, by a man named Leo, who calls himself "notary and sinner." But the original treatise, of which it was a copy, must have been composed before the end of the first century, or at the latest very early in the second. It is therefore one of the oldest books connected with the Christian religion.

We have no means of discovering who was its author. As to the sources of his information, there is no evidence that he was acquainted with any of the New Testament writings except the Gospels of St Matthew and St Luke. For the rest he drew upon the oral tradition, as the synoptic writers had done before him, and upon his own personal experiences of Christian worship and practice. Many of his quotations are not found elsewhere. These may have been taken from some document now lost, or more probably from the "tradition."

The Didache consists of sixteen short chapters, and its contents may be classified as follows.

(1) Chapters i.-vi., Rules for the Christian life. (2) Chapters vii.-xv., Rules for the life of the Christian community in regard to fasting, baptism, the eucharist, prayer, and the ministry. (3) Remarks upon the second coming of Christ —which all the early Christians believed to be imminent.

I will give you a few extracts. "Two ways there are, one of life and one of death. The way of life is this: First, thou shalt love the God who made thee; secondly, thy neighbour as thyself." This is then explained and enforced by a number of quotations, or seeming quotations. For example, "Bless them that curse you; pray for your enemies; fast for them that persecute you. To every one that asketh thee give and ask not back." "But it hath also been said concerning this matter, let thine alms sweat in thy hands until thou knowest to whom thou shouldst give." This seems to mean, let thine alms stick to thine hands till thou knowest that thou oughtest to give—that giving will be for the good of the recipient. Already it had been discovered that Christ could not have intended to command indiscriminate charity, which always does more harm than good. Then the writer goes on to enumerate the commandments of the decalogue, with additions and amplifications. For example: "Thou shalt not kill. Thou shalt not be double-minded nor double-tongued. Thou shalt hate no man; but some thou shalt reprove, and for some thou shalt pray, and some thou shalt love above thy life. My child, flee from every evil thing, and from everything like it. Be not prone to anger, for anger leadeth to murder. Become not a liar, since lying leadeth to theft. Become not a murmurer, since it leadeth to blasphemy. In the Church thou shalt confess thy transgressions, and shalt not draw near for thy prayer with an evil conscience. This is the way of life."

"But the way of death is this. Murders, adulteries, lusts, fornications, thefts, idolatries, magic arts, sorceries, robberies, false testimonies, hypocrisies, duplicity, craft, arrogance, malice, self-will, greed, foul speech, jealousy, over-boldness, haughtiness, pretence, persecutors of the good, hating truth, loving falsehood, knowing not the reward of righteousness, not cleaving to the good, on the watch for evil, far from whom are meekness and patience, loving vanities, pursuing revenge, not pitying the poor, not toiling for one in distress, not knowing Him that made them, murderers of children, destroyers of God's workmanship, turning away from the needy, oppressing the afflicted, advocates of the rich, lawless judges of the poor, universal sinners. May ye be delivered, children, from all these. If thou art able to bear the whole yoke of the Lord, ye shall be perfect; but if thou art not able, what thou art able, that do."

In chapter vii. and onwards, the author proceeds to give rules for the observance of baptism, the eucharist, and fasting. This little treatise forms a transition between the extreme simplicity of Christ's directions and the complicated ceremonies of the later Church. "If thou hast not living water, baptise in other water; and if thou canst not in cold, then in warm. Before the baptism, let the baptiser and the baptised both fast. But let not your fastings be in common with the hypocrites; for they fast on the second day of the week and on the fifth, but do ye fast during the fourth. Thus pray: 'Our Father who art in heaven,' &c. Three times in the day pray ye thus." Then follow prayers and thanksgivings to be used at the eucharist, including one strange sentence, "Before all things we thank thee that thou art mighty."

In chapter xi. our author proceeds to give regulations as to the various kinds of ministers then recognised in the Christian Church. "Every apostle who cometh to you, let him be received as the Lord. But when the apostle departeth, let him take nothing except bread enough till he lodge again: but if he ask money, he is a false prophet. Not every one that speaketh in the spirit is a prophet, but only if he have the ways of the Lord. Son, from their ways shall the false prophet and the true prophet be known. Every true prophet, who will settle among you, is worthy of his support. Likewise a true teacher, he also is worthy like a workman of his support. Every first-fruit then, of the products of the wine-press and threshing-floor, of oxen and of sheep, thou shalt give to the prophets, for they are your high priests. But if ye have no prophet, give it to the poor. On the Lord's day do ye assemble and break bread and give thanks, after confessing your sins, that your sacrifices may be pure. But every one that hath a controversy with his friend, let him not come together with you until they be reconciled, that your sacrifices may not be profaned.

"Appoint for yourselves bishops and deacons worthy of the Lord, men meek and not avaricious, and upright and proved. Your prayers and your alms and all your deeds, so do as ye have it in the gospel of the Lord."

In the sixteenth chapter the writer concludes by speaking of the expected millennium. "Watch for your lives' sake; let your lamps not go out, and your loins not be loosed; for ye know not the hour in which our Lord cometh. Ye shall come together often and seek the things which befit your souls; for the whole time of your faith thus far will not profit you, if ye be not made perfect in the last time. For in the last days the prophets and corruptors shall be multiplied, and the sheep shall be turned into wolves, and love shall be turned into hate; and then shall appear the world-deceiver as the Son of God, and shall do signs and wonders, and the earth shall be given into his hands. Thus shall all created men come into the fire of trial; and many shall be made to stumble and shall perish. But they that endure in their faith shall be saved from under even this curse. And then shall appear the signs of truth; first the sign of an opening in heaven; then the sign of a trumpet's sound; and thirdly, the resurrection of the dead; yet not of all, but as it hath been said, 'the Lord shall come and all the saints with Him.' Then shall the world see the Lord coming upon the clouds of heaven."

I am sorry that the Didache was not recognised as canonical by the early Church. If it had been, it would have formed part of our present Bible. And though it does not contain anything particularly fresh, it would have served to emphasise the practical nature of Christianity, which has been for so many hundreds of years more or less ignored and forgotten. The teaching of the twelve apostles is as free from dogma as the synoptic gospels; and though a little more stress is laid on the sacraments and on fasting than would seem to have been done by Christ Himself, still conduct is everywhere regarded as of supreme and all-comprehensive importance. The two ways —the way of life and the way of death—are distinguished, not by the different creeds and rituals of those who follow them, but by a difference in their conduct. Canon Spence in his interesting little book upon the subject says, rather naïvely, without seeing the full meaning of his admission, — "Some notable omissions characterise the teaching. We find no clear-cut statement as to Christ's relationship to the Father. Nothing is said respecting the atonement or the work of the precious blood. The Holy Spirit, the third Person in the ever-blessed Trinity, is only mentioned twice. His work and office are left unnoticed." Well, these are precisely the "notable omissions" which characterise the synoptic gospels. The fact is, the nearer we get to the time of Christ, the more do we find that dogma disappears, the more does ritual become simple and of quite secondary importance.

My High Church friends believe in antiquity; so do I. They pay great deference to the authority of the early Church; so do I. I find fault with them, not for believing too much in antiquity, but for believing in it too little; not for paying more deference than they should to the early Church, but for paying less. The fact is, their antiquity is comparatively modern, their early Church is a somewhat late modification of original Christianity. They are the victims of a strange hallucination. They think that, in order to understand the mind of Christ, they must betake themselves, not to His contemporaries, but to writers who flourished three or four centuries after He was dead. Whereas to any ordinary human being, to any one whose mental balance has not been disturbed by the peculiar logic of theologians, it is evident that the Founder of a religion must have been Himself the best judge of what He intended His religion to include. The earliest, and the truest, exposition of Christianity is that contained in the synoptic gospels. Whoever will study them in an unbiassed manner will be driven irresistibly to the conclusion that Christ did not wish to establish a religion of creed, that He did not wish to establish a religion of ritual. Christ's Christianity is entirely and exclusively a religion of conduct. Broad Churchism a modern innovation! Why, Broad Churchmen belong to the oldest party in the Church. Broad Churchism is neither more nor less than primitive Christianity.

THE END.

PRINTED BY WILLIAM BLACKWOOD AND SONS.

WORKS BY PROFESSOR MOMERIE.

I.

PERSONALITY;

THE BEGINNING AND END OF METAPHYSICS,

AND A NECESSARY ASSUMPTION IN ALL POSITIVE PHILOSOPHY.

Fourth Edition, revised.   Crown 8vo, 3s.

"This is a little book, but it contains more sound philosophy than many pretentious treatises....... In an admirably lucid way the author scatters to the winds the baseless assumptions of the sense philosophy."—*British Quarterly Review.*

"It is not often that we have to complain of the brevity of a sermon or of a treatise on philosophy; but in the case of a little book of the latter kind, recently published anonymously, we have found the arguments so cogent, the style so clear, and the matter at issue so important, that we heartily wish that the writer had allowed himself room for the fuller treatment of his subject....... We confidently refer our readers to this well-reasoned volume."—*Modern Review.*

"Professor Momerie's remarks on the doctrines of the defenders of empiricism present a close, and thoroughly scientific, examination of the views these thinkers put forth as to the nature of sensation, perception, and cognition....... The arguments are throughout conducted with marked logical power, and the conclusions are very important in relation to the present aspect of philosophical thought in England."—*Scotsman.*

"The work under our notice will well repay the careful reading of those who wish to have at their command plain answers to modern positivism."—*Ecclesiastical Gazette.*

"His discussion of these questions stamps Dr Momerie as an acute metaphysician, a philosophical scholar, and a powerful dialectician."—*Glasgow Herald.*

"When published anonymously received a very hearty welcome by all who were interested in the advent of a new writer of great power, of happy diction, and of independent thinking."—*Montrose Standard.*

WILLIAM BLACKWOOD & SONS, EDINBURGH AND LONDON.

And all Booksellers.

II.

THE ORIGIN OF EVIL;

AND OTHER SERMONS.

Sixth Edition. Crown 8vo, 5s.

"Professor Momerie has done well to publish his sermons; they are good reading.......A real contribution to the side of common-sense religion."—*Saturday Review.*

"We decidedly recommend them to persons perplexed by the speculations of modern science."—*Spectator.*

"This is a remarkable volume of sermons. Though it consists of only about 300 pages, it contains an amount of thought and learning which might have been expanded into a bulky folio."—*Glasgow Mail.*

"These sermons are some of the very best produced in this country within the last hundred years."—*Inquirer.*

"The author is an original thinker, whose sympathies are very wide."—*Guardian.*

"Those who preach may learn much from their perusal."—*Christian World.*

"Out of the common run, they give one a refreshing sense of novelty and power."—*Glasgow Herald.*

"Die Vorträge zeigen allenthalben eine schöne Harmonie zwischen Schriftwahrheit und Lebenswahrheit."—*Deutsches Litteraturblatt.*

"Der Verfasser behandelt in diesen Vorträgen wichtige Fragen aus dem Gebiet des christlichen Lebens. Wir heben besonders die über das Leiden hervor, in denen der Verfasser tiefe beherzigenswerthe Gedanken ausspricht. Wir nehmen keinen Anstand, diese Vorträge zum Besten zu rechnen, was über diesen Gegenstand gesagt worden."—*Christliches Bücherschatz.*

"The author of the 'Origin of Evil' will go sadly astray if he does not make his mark on the age."—*London Figaro.*

"We should almost like to have heard these sermons preached. We are willing to read them carefully, and recommend them to others for like reading, even though, in almost every instance, we dissent from the author's pleading."—*National Reformer.*

"These sermons are everything that sermons ought *not* to be."—*English Independent.*

III.

DEFECTS OF MODERN CHRISTIANITY;

AND OTHER SERMONS.

Third Edition. Crown 8vo, 5s.

"Throughout Mr Momerie's attractive little volume the morning air of the new world breathes through the dry leaves of the old theology."—*Westminster Review.*

"There is an intellectuality, spirituality, and a simplicity in Mr Momerie's sermons, that should make them models for young preachers."—*Christian Union.*

"Professor Momerie, by his former books, has already laid the foundation of a reputation as a philosophical thinker and an able expositor of religious subjects. The present volume is marked by equal ability, intellectual force, independent and original thinking, and will confirm the favourable opinion which he has already produced.......Whatever views readers may detect as different from their own, they will not fail to admire the author's powerful enforcement of the practical side of Christianity.......There follows, as the second part of the volume, nine lectures on the Book of Job; and we have not read before, within the same compass, a more masterly and interesting exposition of that great poem.......There are also three admirable sermons on 'The Connection between Reason and Faith,' which will repay repeated reading.......The volume deserves to be widely read; and whether readers agree or not in all respects with the author, they will not rise from the perusal without feeling that Christianity is something grander than they have ordinarily realised it to be, and that the Christian life is the bravest and most beautiful life possible."—*Aberdeen Journal.*

"Very fresh and striking."—*Globe.*

"Although he is a polished and accomplished scholar, he simply defies the conventionalities of churches and schools."—*Literary World.*

IV.

THE BASIS OF RELIGION;

BEING AN EXAMINATION OF 'NATURAL RELIGION.'

Second Edition. Crown 8vo, 2s. 6d.

"As a controversialist, Professor Momerie is no less candid than he is remorselessly severe."—*Scotsman.*

"As a revelation of the pretentiousness of that philosophy [Positivism] Dr Momerie's powerful essay is very valuable."—*Fifeshire Journal.*

"The result of profound study and earnest thought.......This attempt to sketch out a basis for rational theology is fitted to the needs of the times. ......Professor Momerie has won for himself a name as one of the most powerful and original thinkers of the day."—*Globe.*

"Professor Momerie has wide views of men and things, resembling in this quality the author of 'Ecce Homo' himself, and he has attacked from the Cambridge University pulpit the book 'Natural Religion,' accusing it of considerable vagueness of conception and of considerable misconception of critical points of its own argument. The present book presents the substance of these sermons in the form of a brief essay.......We would recommend our readers to see for themselves how those confusions of thought, by which the school of writers—of whom the author of 'Natural Religion' is an eminent representative—seek to save religion when supernaturalism has disappeared, are exposed. We are certain they will be charmed with the accurate philosophical thinking of Professor Momerie, with his unpretentious display of keen logical reasoning, conveyed in lucid and forcible language, which arrays and adorns it like a well-fitting garment."—*Eskdale Advertiser.*

"Greater force is given to this essay, since the author is himself an advanced thinker."—*Christian Union.*

V.

AGNOSTICISM.

Third Edition. Crown 8vo, 5s.

"To readers who do not demand that 'the scheme of salvation in its fulness' should be enunciated in every sermon, this volume, which is happily free from rhetoric, and for the most part from any ostentation of the reading which it indicates, will be interesting from its acuteness, learning, and insight."—*Saturday Review.*

"This is a really good book. It is profound in thought, large and comprehensive in view, liberal in spirit, and delightfully clear and simple in style. We wish that theologians and philosophers in general would write in Professor Momerie's manner.......Following the chapters on Agnosticism, there are ten other chapters on the book of Ecclesiastes. They form an admirable and scholarly analysis of that strange and melancholy book."—*The Inquirer.*

"We are thankful for so masterly, so comprehensive, and so complete a vindication of the principles of Christian Theism, with its powerful refutation of the main positions of Agnosticism. The book meets a real and widespread need, in a style as trenchant and effective as it is popular."—*Freeman.*

"Dr Momerie's breadth of intellect and sympathy, his clear thinking and well-chastened style, as well as his deep religiousness, which will, no doubt, after a time assume a more positively evangelical form, eminently adapt him to be a teacher to his generation. He has freed himself, by we know not what process, from many of the prejudices of the older schools; but he can search into the very soul of unbelieving sophistry, and the spirit of his exhortation is always ennobling and heavenward."—*Methodist Times.*

"It is long since we have met with a volume of sermons which will so well repay a careful study."—*Ecclesiastical Gazette.*

"The work of a majestic intellect."—*Fifeshire Journal.*

VI.

PREACHING AND HEARING;

AND OTHER SERMONS.

Second Edition. Crown 8vo, 4s. 6d.

"The author, himself one of the most eloquent preachers of the day, is eminently qualified to do justice to his subject. He has brought to it an experience and scholarly proficiency which few men could have done."—*Christian Union.*

"For such preaching as this, and for all the ample learning and wise thought by which it is fortified, the Church of God has every reason to be thankful."—*Literary World.*

"Marked by all the force, acuteness, and eloquence which we have learnt to expect from him, and in addition by a knowledge of men and manners not generally associated with philosophical research.......His literary style is another proof, if proof were needed, of the vast resources of the simple Anglo-Saxon."—*Fifeshire Journal.*

"His sermons are unlike any sermons we can call to mind."—*Guardian.*

"If such sermons were often to be heard from the pulpit, preachers would not have to complain of empty pews or inattentive listeners."—*Rock.*

"Their delivery was quite startling."—*Swansea Journal.*

"Those who would know what pulpit boldness in the present day really means should make these sermons their study."—*Christian World.*

"The present volume is more directly popular in style, and amply maintains the reputation of the writer."—*Inquirer.*

VII.

BELIEF IN GOD.

Second Edition. Crown 8vo, 3s.

"One of the most brilliant arguments for the Divine existence."—*Christian World.*

"In some respects Professor Momerie is the ablest preacher of his day. ......He is ever endeavouring to present recondite problems in the simplest, clearest language, and in this he is eminently successful.......It is not too abstruse even for mere smatterers in philosophical discussion. Considering its scope, it is indeed astonishingly lucid."—*Dundee Advertiser.*

"No preacher need be ashamed to face the most scientific sceptic with this little book in his hand."—*Literary World.*

"From the time that Professor Momerie published anonymously the volume on 'The Origin of Evil,' his writings have been devoured with exceptional keenness by intelligent readers. Many were the conjectures as to who the author of that work was, but it was universally allowed that the anonymous writer was destined to leave his mark upon the mind of the country: he was a daring and fresh thinker, and was possessed of rare unravelling power. This little volume bears the impress of his majestic intellect....... It is a model of lucid style, clear and consecutive reasoning, fairness to an honourable opponent, and humility in victory."—*Perthshire Advertiser.*

"'Belief in God' was originally written for the 'Helps to Belief' Series, but the editor, thinking it too abstruse, recommended considerable alterations. We are devoutly thankful the gifted Professor refused to mutilate his work, and withdrew it from the series."—*Nonconformist.*

"His criticism of Herbert Spencer's theory of the Unknowable is very acute."—*Glasgow Herald.*

"It is spread out into only eighty pages, but those eighty pages contain more material for thought than many another volume or series of volumes contain in eight hundred."—*Inquirer.*

VIII.

INSPIRATION;

AND OTHER SERMONS.

Second Edition.　　Crown 8vo, 5s.

"Canon Liddon, preaching last Sunday afternoon in St Paul's Cathedral, declared that it would be difficult to maintain the authority of Christ as a teacher of religious truth if the Book of Daniel were written in the second, and not in the sixth century B.C. Statements of this kind are as deplorable as they are unwarranted....... A happier and a wiser method of dealing with the relations of science and criticism to the Scriptures has been adopted by Professor Momerie in his new volume."—*Christian World.*

"The gifted Professor has broken at many points with rigid orthodoxy. He is a Broad Churchman of the Broad Churchmen. But his very breadth and catholicity of view, the unswerving steadfastness of his search after truth, and his gift of powerful expression, make him an ally whom even the narrowest sticklers for the faith without change cannot be blind enough to throw over."—*Fifeshire Journal.*

"The sermons on 'Pessimism' constitute a treatise in themselves."—*Irish Ecclesiastical Gazette.*

"The abilities of Dr Momerie, and his services with respect to those questions in which the spheres of religion and philosophy touch, are well known; and there is much in the present volume that will repay attentive perusal. The treatment of pessimism leaves nothing to be desired."—*Saturday Review.*

"Professor Momerie's latest volume fully bears out his reputation for originality, vigour, and lucidity."—*John Bull.*

"A unique contribution to the literature of the day."—*Lady's Pictorial.*

"Here is a bold note, boldly struck; it is only one of many in the book that deserve the attention of opponents as well as friends, and that only a brave man dared touch."—*Scottish Leader.*

"In the course of this remarkable book he passes in review many of the doctrinal questions which are now agitating the Church, and gives a rational explanation of some of the difficulties that perplex both young and old students of theology."—*Dundee Advertiser.*

"Professor Momerie has approached his work with a mental penetration and spiritual devotion worthy of so distinguished a Biblical scholar. The initial chapter, which discusses 'The Evolution of the Bible,' is a masterly exposition. There is a freshness and potency in the author's thought and reasoning that both charm and convince."—*Christian Union.*

IX.

CHURCH AND CREED.

Second Edition. Crown 8vo, 4s. 6d.

"I cannot say that I am in the habit of reading many sermons. But I did read 'Church and Creed,' and I can recommend them to all those desirous of allying religion with common-sense."—*Truth*.

"Persons who still retain the old-fashioned notion that an ordained clergyman holds, in some sense, a brief for the defence, will be bewildered by this wholesale tearing to pieces of dogmas and creeds; and many more, while admiring much in the sermons themselves, will probably take exception, not so much to what is said as to where it is said. 'Church and Creed,' however, is a remarkable book, and a sign of the times which will be noted with different feelings by various classes of thinkers."—*Life*.

"Original, fearless, reverent criticism."—*Yorkshire Post*.

"Simple yet masterly."—*Lincolnshire Free Press*.

"The discourses, one and all, in the volume before us are indeed works of art."—*Glasgow Herald*.

"His lessons on self-sacrifice are well worth careful attention."—*Ecclesiastical Gazette*.

"Dr Momerie is a law unto himself, and is a great illustration of the freedom of thought allowed in the English pulpit. Take for example the sermon in the present volume, entitled 'The Gods of the Bible,' and see what a new face it puts upon our cherished notions of a uniform deistic belief. The whole of the present volume overflows with similar dry, fearless, decisive, almost caustic enunciations that cut athwart hereditary faiths, and it requires a strong mind to follow the preacher as he advances from one startling proposition to another."—*Irish Ecclesiastical Gazette*.

"It is this cheerful and healthful view of life, combined with a hatred of all bigotry and narrowness, that makes Professor Momerie's sermons the inspiration that crowded congregations find them. The man who can persuade people in these pessimistic days that God meant them to laugh and enjoy the life He has given them, and yet be in the truest sense of the word religious, is doing a service to the age which it greatly needs."—*Literary World*.

"It is to be earnestly hoped that the great Head of the Church will raise up an Athanasius in our midst to combat and refute the errors with which it abounds."—*Newbery House Magazine*.

WILLIAM BLACKWOOD & SONS, EDINBURGH AND LONDON.

And all Booksellers.

IN ONE VOLUME. THE LIBRARY EDITION OF

STORMONTH'S DICTIONARY

OF THE

ENGLISH LANGUAGE,

PRONOUNCING, ETYMOLOGICAL, AND EXPLANATORY.

Embracing Scientific and other Terms, numerous Familiar Terms, and a Copious Selection of Old English Words. To which are appended Lists of Scripture and other Proper Names, Abbreviations, and Foreign Words and Phrases.

BY THE REV. JAMES STORMONTH.

The PRONUNCIATION carefully revised by the Rev. P. H. PHELP, M.A. CANTAB.

Royal 8vo, handsomely bound in half-morocco, 31s. 6d.

Opinions of the British and American Press.

Times.—"This may serve in great measure the purposes of an English cyclopedia. It gives lucid and succinct definitions of the technical terms in science and art, in law and medicine. We have the explanation of words and phrases that puzzle most people, showing wonderfully comprehensive and out-of-the-way research. . . . We need only add, that the dictionary appears in all its departments to have been brought down to meet the latest demands of the day, and that it is admirably printed."

Pall Mall Gazette.—"The pronunciation of every word is given, the symbols employed for marking the sounds being commendably clear. . . . After the pronunciation comes the etymology. It has, we think, been well managed here. And the matter is, on the whole, as judiciously chosen as it is skilfully compressed and arranged."

Scotsman.—"There can be no question that the work when completed will form one of the best and most serviceable works of reference of its class. . . . It is admirably adapted to meet the requirements of every ordinary reader, and there are few occasions of special reference to which it will not be found adequate. The definitions are necessarily brief, but they are almost always clear and pointed. . . . A word of praise is due to the beauty and clearness of the printing."

STORMONTH'S DICTIONARY—*Continued.*

Opinions of the British and American Press—*Continued.*

Civil Service Gazette.—"We have had occasion to notice the peculiar features and merits of 'Stormonth's Dictionary,' and we need not repeat our commendations both of the judicious plan and the admirable execution. . . . This is a pre-eminently good, comprehensive, and authentic English lexicon, embracing not only all the words to be found in previous dictionaries, but all the modern words—scientific, new coined, and adopted from foreign languages, and now naturalised and legitimised."

Notes and Queries.—"The whole constitutes a work of high utility."

Dublin Irish Times.—"The book has the singular merit of being a dictionary of the highest order in every department and in every arrangement, without being cumbersome; whilst for ease of reference there is no dictionary we know of that equals it. . . . For the library table it is also, we must repeat, precisely the sort of volume required, and indispensable to every large reader or literary worker."

Liverpool Mercury.—"Every page bears the evidence of extensive scholarship and laborious research, nothing necessary to the elucidation of present-day language being omitted. . . . As a book of reference for terms in every department of English speech, this work must be accorded a high place—in fact, it is quite a library in itself. . . . It is a marvel of accuracy."

New York Tribune.—"The work exhibits all the freshness and best results of modern lexicographic scholarship, and is arranged with great care, so as to facilitate reference."

New York Mail and Express.—"Is the nearest approach to the ideal popular dictionary that has yet appeared in our language."

New York Sun.—"A well-planned and carefully-executed work, which has decided merits of its own, and for which there is a place not filled by any of its rivals."

Boston Journal.—"A critical and accurate dictionary, the embodiment of good scholarship, and the result of modern researches. . . . It holds an unrivalled place in bringing forth the result of modern philological criticism."

Boston Gazette.—"There can be but little doubt that, when completed, the work will be one of the most serviceable and most accurate that English lexicography has yet produced for general use"

Toronto Globe.—"In every respect this is one of the best works of the kind in the language."

WILLIAM BLACKWOOD & SONS, EDINBURGH AND LONDON.

CATALOGUE

OF

MESSRS BLACKWOOD & SONS' PUBLICATIONS.

PHILOSOPHICAL CLASSICS FOR ENGLISH READERS.
EDITED BY WILLIAM KNIGHT, LL.D.,
Professor of Moral Philosophy in the University of St Andrews.

In crown 8vo Volumes, with Portraits, price 3s. 6d.

Now ready—

DESCARTES, by Professor Mahaffy, Dublin.—BUTLER, by Rev. W. Lucas Collins, M.A.—BERKELEY, by Professor Campbell Fraser, Edinburgh.—FICHTE, by Professor Adamson, Owens College, Manchester.—KANT, by Professor Wallace, Oxford.—HAMILTON, by Professor Veitch, Glasgow.—HEGEL, by Professor Edward Caird, Glasgow.—LEIBNIZ, by J. Theodore Merz.—VICO, by Professor Flint, Edinburgh.—HOBBES, by Professor Croom Robertson, London.—HUME, by the Editor.—SPINOZA, by the Very Rev. Principal Caird, Glasgow.—BACON: Part I. The Life, by Professor Nichol, Glasgow.—BACON: Part II. Philosophy, by the same Author.

In preparation.

LOCKE, by Professor Campbell Fraser, Edinburgh. [*Immediately.*
MILL, by the Right Hon. A. J. Balfour.

FOREIGN CLASSICS FOR ENGLISH READERS.
EDITED BY MRS OLIPHANT.

In crown 8vo, 2s. 6d.

Contents of the Series.

DANTE, by the Editor.—VOLTAIRE, by Lieut.-General Sir E. B. Hamley, K.C.B.—PASCAL, by Principal Tulloch.—PETRARCH, by Henry Reeve, C.B.—GOETHE, By A. Hayward, Q.C.—MOLIÈRE, by the Editor and F. Tarver, M.A.—MONTAIGNE, by Rev. W. L. Collins, M.A.—RABELAIS, by Walter Besant, M.A.—CALDERON, by E. J. Hasell.—SAINT SIMON, by Clifton W. Collins, M.A.—CERVANTES, by the Editor.—CORNEILLE AND RACINE, by Henry M. Trollope.—MADAME DE SÉVIGNÉ, by Miss Thackeray.—LA FONTAINE, AND OTHER FRENCH FABULISTS, by Rev. W. Lucas Collins, M.A.—SCHILLER, by James Sime, M.A., Author of 'Lessing, his Life and Writings.'—TASSO, by E. J. Hasell.—ROUSSEAU, by Henry Grey Graham.

ALFRED DE MUSSET. *In preparation.*

Now Complete.

ANCIENT CLASSICS FOR ENGLISH READERS.
EDITED BY THE REV. W. LUCAS COLLINS, M.A.

Complete in 28 Vols. crown 8vo, cloth, price 2s. 6d. each. And may also be had in 14 Volumes, strongly and neatly bound, with calf or vellum back, £3, 10s.

Contents of the Series.

HOMER: THE ILIAD, by the Editor.—HOMER: THE ODYSSEY, by the Editor.—HERODOTUS, by George C. Swayne, M.A.—XENOPHON, by Sir Alexander Grant, Bart., LL.D.—EURIPIDES, by W. B. Donne.—ARISTOPHANES, by the Editor.—PLATO, by Clifton W. Collins, M.A.—LUCIAN, by the Editor.—ÆSCHYLUS, by the Right Rev. the Bishop of Colombo.—SOPHOCLES, by Clifton W. Collins, M.A.—HESIOD AND THEOGNIS, by the Rev. J. Davies, M.A.—GREEK ANTHOLOGY, by Lord Neaves.—VIRGIL, by the Editor.—HORACE, by Sir Theodore Martin, K.C.B.—JUVENAL, by Edward Walford, M.A.—PLAUTUS AND TERENCE, by the Editor.—THE COMMENTARIES OF CÆSAR, by Anthony Trollope.—TACITUS, by W. B. Donne.—CICERO, by the Editor.—PLINY'S LETTERS, by the Rev. Alfred Church, M.A., and the Rev. W. J. Brodribb, M.A.—LIVY, by the Editor.—OVID, by the Rev. A. Church, M.A.—CATULLUS, TIBULLUS, AND PROPERTIUS, by the Rev. Jas. Davies, M.A.—DEMOSTHENES, by the Rev. W. J. Brodribb, M.A.—ARISTOTLE, by Sir Alexander Grant, Bart., LL.D.—THUCYDIDES, by the Editor.—LUCRETIUS, by W. H. Mallock, M.A.—PINDAR, by the Rev. F. D. Morice, M.A.

Saturday Review.—"It is difficult to estimate too highly the value of such a series as this in giving 'English readers' an insight, exact as far as it goes, into those olden times which are so remote and yet to many of us so close."

CATALOGUE

OF

MESSRS BLACKWOOD & SONS'

PUBLICATIONS.

ALISON. History of Europe. By Sir ARCHIBALD ALISON, BART., D.C.L.
  1. From the Commencement of the French Revolution to the Battle of Waterloo.
      LIBRARY EDITION, 14 vols., with Portraits. Demy 8vo, £10, 10s.
      ANOTHER EDITION, in 20 vols. crown 8vo, £6.
      PEOPLE'S EDITION, 13 vols. crown 8vo, £2, 11s.
  2. Continuation to the Accession of Louis Napoleon.
      LIBRARY EDITION, 8 vols. 8vo, £6, 7s. 6d.
      PEOPLE'S EDITION, 8 vols. crown 8vo, 34s.
  3. Epitome of Alison's History of Europe. Twenty-ninth Thousand, 7s. 6d.
  4. Atlas to Alison's History of Europe. By A. Keith Johnston.
      LIBRARY EDITION, demy 4to, £3, 3s.
      PEOPLE'S EDITION, 31s. 6d.

——— Life of John Duke of Marlborough. With some Account of his Contemporaries, and of the War of the Succession. Third Edition, 2 vols. 8vo. Portraits and Maps, 30s.

——— Essays: Historical, Political, and Miscellaneous. 3 vols. demy 8vo, 45s.

ACTA SANCTORUM HIBERNIÆ; Ex Codice Salmanticensi. Nunc primum integre edita opera CAROLI DE SMEDT et JOSEPHI DE BACKER, e Soc. Jesu, Hagiographorum Bollandianorum; Auctore et Sumptus Largiente JOANNE PATRICIO MARCHIONE BOTHAE. In One handsome 4to Volume, bound in half roxburghe, £2, 2s.; in paper wrapper, 31s. 6d.

AIRD. Poetical Works of Thomas Aird. Fifth Edition, with Memoir of the Author by the Rev. JARDINE WALLACE, and Portrait. Crown 8vo, 7s. 6d.

ALLARDYCE. The City of Sunshine. By ALEXANDER ALLARDYCE. Three vols. post 8vo, £1, 5s. 6d.

——— Memoir of the Honourable George Keith Elphinstone, K.B., Viscount Keith of Stonehaven, Marischal, Admiral of the Red. 8vo, with Portrait, Illustrations, and Maps, 21s.

ALMOND. Sermons by a Lay Head-master. By HELY HUTCHINSON ALMOND, M.A. Oxon., Head-master of Loretto School. Crown 8vo, 5s.

ANCIENT CLASSICS FOR ENGLISH READERS. Edited by Rev. W. LUCAS COLLINS, M.A. Price 2s. 6d. each. *For list of Volumes, see page 2.*

AYTOUN. Lays of the Scottish Cavaliers, and other Poems. By W. EDMONDSTOUNE AYTOUN, D.C.L., Professor of Rhetoric and Belles-Lettres in the University of Edinburgh. New Edition, printed from a new type, and tastefully bound. Fcap. 8vo, 3s. 6d.

Another Edition, being the Thirtieth. Fcap. 8vo, cloth extra, 7s. 6d.

Cheap Edition. Fcap. 8vo. Illustrated Cover. Price 1s.

—— An Illustrated Edition of the Lays of the Scottish Cavaliers. From designs by Sir NOEL PATON. Small 4to, in gilt cloth, 21s.

—— Bothwell: a Poem. Third Edition. Fcap., 7s. 6d.

—— Poems and Ballads of Goethe. Translated by Professor AYTOUN and Sir THEODORE MARTIN, K.C.B. Third Edition. Fcap., 6s.

—— Bon Gaultier's Book of Ballads. By the SAME. Fifteenth and Cheaper Edition. With Illustrations by Doyle, Leech, and Crowquill. Fcap. 8vo, 5s.

—— The Ballads of Scotland. Edited by Professor AYTOUN. Fourth Edition. 2 vols. fcap. 8vo, 12s.

—— Memoir of William E. Aytoun, D.C.L. By Sir THEODORE MARTIN, K.C.B. With Portrait. Post 8vo, 12s.

BACH. On Musical Education and Vocal Culture. By ALBERT B. BACH. Fourth Edition. 8vo, 7s. 6d.

—— The Principles of Singing. A Practical Guide for Vocalists and Teachers. With Course of Vocal Exercises. Crown 8vo, 6s.

—— The Art of Singing. With Musical Exercises for Young People. Crown 8vo, 3s.

BALLADS AND POEMS. By MEMBERS OF THE GLASGOW BALLAD CLUB. Crown 8vo, 7s. 6d.

BANNATYNE. Handbook of Republican Institutions in the United States of America. Based upon Federal and State Laws, and other reliable sources of information. By DUGALD J. BANNATYNE, Scotch Solicitor, New York; Member of the Faculty of Procurators, Glasgow. Cr. 8vo, 7s. 6d.

BELLAIRS. The Transvaal War, 1880-81. Edited by Lady BELLAIRS. With a Frontispiece and Map. 8vo, 15s.

—— Gossips with Girls and Maidens, Betrothed and Free. New Edition. Crown 8vo, 5s.

BESANT. The Revolt of Man. By WALTER BESANT, M.A. Eighth Edition. Crown 8vo, 3s. 6d.

—— Readings in Rabelais. Crown 8vo, 7s. 6d.

BEVERIDGE. Culross and Tulliallan; or Perthshire on Forth. Its History and Antiquities. With Elucidations of Scottish Life and Character from the Burgh and Kirk-Session Records of that District. By DAVID BEVERIDGE. 2 vols. 8vo, with Illustrations, 42s.

—— Between the Ochils and the Forth; or, From Stirling Bridge to Aberdour. Crown 8vo, 6s.

BLACK. Heligoland and the Islands of the North Sea. By WILLIAM GEORGE BLACK. Crown 8vo, 4s.

BLACKIE. Lays and Legends of Ancient Greece. By JOHN STUART BLACKIE, Emeritus Professor of Greek in the University of Edinburgh. Second Edition. Fcap. 8vo. 5s.

—— The Wisdom of Goethe. Fcap. 8vo. Cloth, extra gilt, 6s.

—— Scottish Song: Its Wealth, Wisdom, and Social Significance. Crown 8vo. With Music. 7s. 6d.

—— A Song of Heroes. Crown 8vo, 6s.

BLACKWOOD'S MAGAZINE, from Commencement in 1817 to February 1890. Nos. 1 to 892, forming 145 Volumes.

—— Index to Blackwood's Magazine. Vols. 1 to 50. 8vo, 15s.

BLACKWOOD. Tales from Blackwood. Forming Twelve Volumes of Interesting and Amusing Railway Reading. Price One Shilling each, in Paper Cover. Sold separately at all Railway Bookstalls.
They may also be had bound in cloth, 18s., and in half calf, richly gilt, 30s.
Or 12 volumes in 6, roxburghe, 21s., and half red morocco, 28s.

—— Tales from Blackwood. New Series. Complete in Twenty-four Shilling Parts. Handsomely bound in 12 vols., cloth, 30s. In leather back, roxburghe style, 37s. 6d. In half calf, gilt, 52s. 6d. In half morocco, 55s.
In course of Publication.

—— Tales from Blackwood. Third Series. In Parts. Each price 1s. [Nos. I. to VII. now ready.
In course of Publication.

—— Travel, Adventure, and Sport. From 'Blackwood's Magazine.' In Parts. Uniform with 'Tales from Blackwood.' Each price 1s.
[Nos. I. to VI. now ready.

—— Standard Novels. Uniform in size and legibly Printed. Each Novel complete in one volume.

FLORIN SERIES, Illustrated Boards. Or in New Cloth Binding, 2s. 6d.

Tom Cringle's Log. By Michael Scott.
The Cruise of the Midge. By the Same.
Cyril Thornton. By Captain Hamilton.
Annals of the Parish. By John Galt.
The Provost, &c. By John Galt.
Sir Andrew Wylie. By John Galt.
The Entail. By John Galt.
Miss Molly. By Beatrice May Butt.
Reginald Dalton. By J. G. Lockhart.

Pen Owen. By Dean Hook.
Adam Blair. By J. G. Lockhart.
Lady Lee's Widowhood. By General Sir E. B. Hamley.
Salem Chapel. By Mrs Oliphant.
The Perpetual Curate. By Mrs Oliphant.
Miss Marjoribanks. By Mrs Oliphant.
John: A Love Story. By Mrs Oliphant.

SHILLING SERIES, Illustrated Cover. Or in New Cloth Binding, 1s. 6d.

The Rector, and The Doctor's Family. By Mrs Oliphant.
The Life of Mansie Wauch. By D. M. Moir.
Peninsular Scenes and Sketches. By F. Hardman.

Sir Frizzle Pumpkin, Nights at Mess, &c.
The Subaltern.
Life in the Far West. By G. F. Ruxton.
Valerius: A Roman Story. By J. G. Lockhart.

BLACKMORE. The Maid of Sker. By R. D. Blackmore, Author of 'Lorna Doone,' &c. New Edition. Crown 8vo, 6s.

BLAIR. History of the Catholic Church of Scotland. From the Introduction of Christianity to the Present Day. By Alphons Bellesheim, D.D., Canon of Aix-la-Chapelle. Translated, with Notes and Additions, by D. Oswald Hunter Blair, O.S.B., Monk of Fort Augustus. To be completed in 4 vols. 8vo. Vols. I. and II. 25s. Vol. III. 12s. 6d.

BOSCOBEL TRACTS. Relating to the Escape of Charles the Second after the Battle of Worcester, and his subsequent Adventures. Edited by J. Hughes, Esq., A.M. A New Edition, with additional Notes and Illustrations, including Communications from the Rev. R. H. Barham, Author of the 'Ingoldsby Legends.' 8vo, with Engravings, 16s.

BROUGHAM. Memoirs of the Life and Times of Henry Lord Brougham. Written by Himself. 3 vols. 8vo, £2, 8s. The Volumes are sold separately, price 16s. each.

BROWN. The Forester: A Practical Treatise on the Planting, Rearing, and General Management of Forest-trees. By James Brown, LL.D., Inspector of and Reporter on Woods and Forests. Fifth Edition, revised and enlarged. Royal 8vo, with Engravings, 36s.

BROWN. The Ethics of George Eliot's Works. By John Crombie Brown. Fourth Edition. Crown 8vo, 2s. 6d.

BRYDALL. Art in Scotland; its Origin and Progress. By Robert Brydall, Master of St George's Art School of Glasgow. 8vo, 12s. 6d.

BROWN. A Manual of Botany, Anatomical and Physiological. For the Use of Students. By Robert Brown, M.A., Ph.D. Crown 8vo, with numerous Illustrations, 12s. 6d.

BRUCE. In Clover and Heather. Poems by WALLACE BRUCE. Crown 8vo, 4s. 6d.
  A limited number of Copies on large hand-made paper, 12s. 6d.

BUCHAN. Introductory Text-Book of Meteorology. By ALEXANDER BUCHAN, M.A., F.R.S.E., Secretary of the Scottish Meteorological Society, &c. Crown 8vo, with 8 Coloured Charts and Engravings, 4s. 6d.

BUCHANAN. The Shirè Highlands (East Central Africa). By JOHN BUCHANAN, Planter at Zomba. Crown 8vo, 5s.

BURBIDGE. Domestic Floriculture, Window Gardening, and Floral Decorations. Being practical directions for the Propagation, Culture, and Arrangement of Plants and Flowers as Domestic Ornaments. By F. W. BURBIDGE. Second Edition. Crown 8vo, with numerous Illustrations, 7s. 6d.

——— Cultivated Plants: Their Propagation and Improvement. Including Natural and Artificial Hybridisation, Raising from Seed, Cuttings, and Layers, Grafting and Budding, as applied to the Families and Genera in Cultivation. Crown 8vo, with numerous Illustrations, 12s. 6d.

BURTON. The History of Scotland: From Agricola's Invasion to the Extinction of the last Jacobite Insurrection. By JOHN HILL BURTON, D.C.L., Historiographer-Royal for Scotland. New and Enlarged Edition, 8 vols., and Index. Crown 8vo, £3, 3s.

——— History of the British Empire during the Reign of Queen Anne. In 3 vols. 8vo. 36s.

——— The Scot Abroad. Third Edition. Crown 8vo, 10s. 6d.

——— The Book-Hunter. New Edition. With Portrait. Crown 8vo, 7s. 6d.

BUTE. The Roman Breviary: Reformed by Order of the Holy Œcumenical Council of Trent; Published by Order of Pope St Pius V.; and Revised by Clement VIII. and Urban VIII.; together with the Offices since granted. Translated out of Latin into English by JOHN, Marquess of Bute, K.T. In 2 vols, crown 8vo. cloth boards, edges uncut. £2, 2s.

——— The Altus of St Columba. With a Prose Paraphrase and Notes. In paper cover, 2s. 6d.

BUTLER. Pompeii: Descriptive and Picturesque. By W. BUTLER. Post 8vo, 5s.

BUTT. Miss Molly. By BEATRICE MAY BUTT. Cheap Edition, 2s.

——— Eugenie. Crown 8vo, 6s. 6d.

——— Elizabeth, and Other Sketches. Crown 8vo, 6s.

——— Novels. New and Uniform Edition. Crown 8vo, each 2s. 6d. Delicia. *Now ready.*

CAIRD. Sermons. By JOHN CAIRD, D.D., Principal of the University of Glasgow. Sixteenth Thousand. Fcap. 8vo, 5s.

——— Religion in Common Life. A Sermon preached in Crathie Church, October 14, 1855, before Her Majesty the Queen and Prince Albert. Published by Her Majesty's Command. Cheap Edition, 3d.

CAMPBELL. Sermons Preached before the Queen at Balmoral. By the Rev. A. A. CAMPBELL, Minister of Crathie. Published by Command of Her Majesty. Crown 8vo, 4s. 6d.

CAMPBELL. Records of Argyll. Legends, Traditions, and Recollections of Argyllshire Highlanders, collected chiefly from the Gaelic. With Notes on the Antiquity of the Dress, Clan Colours or Tartans of the Highlanders. By LORD ARCHIBALD CAMPBELL. Illustrated with Nineteen full-page Etchings. 4to, printed on hand-made paper, £3, 3s.

CANTON. A Lost Epic, and other Poems. By WILLIAM CANTON. Crown 8vo, 5s.

CARR. Margaret Maliphant. A Novel. By Mrs COMYNS CARR, Author of 'La Fortunina,' 'North Italian Folk,' &c. 3 vols. post 8vo, 25s. 6d.

CARRICK. Koumiss; or, Fermented Mare's Milk: and its Uses in the Treatment and Cure of Pulmonary Consumption, and other Wasting Diseases. With an Appendix on the best Methods of Fermenting Cow's Milk. By GEORGE L. CARRICK, M.D., L.R.C.S.E. and L.R.C.P.E., Physician to the British Embassy, St Petersburg, &c. Crown 8vo, 10s. 6d.

CAUVIN. A Treasury of the English and German Languages. Compiled from the best Authors and Lexicographers in both Languages. By JOSEPH CAUVIN, LL.D. and Ph.D., of the University of Göttingen, &c. Crown 8vo, 7s. 6d.

CAVE-BROWN. Lambeth Palace and its Associations. By J. CAVE-BROWN, M.A., Vicar of Detling, Kent, and for many years Curate of Lambeth Parish Church. With an Introduction by the Archbishop of Canterbury. Second Edition, containing an additional Chapter on Medieval Life in the Old Palaces. 8vo, with Illustrations, 21s.

CHARTERIS. Canonicity; or, Early Testimonies to the Existence and Use of the Books of the New Testament. Based on Kirchhoffer's 'Quellensammlung.' Edited by A. H. CHARTERIS, D.D., Professor of Biblical Criticism in the University of Edinburgh. 8vo, 18s.

CHRISTISON. Life of Sir Robert Christison, Bart., M.D., D.C.L. Oxon., Professor of Medical Jurisprudence in the University of Edinburgh. Edited by his SONS. In two vols. 8vo. Vol. I.—Autobiography. 16s. Vol. II. —Memoirs. 16s.

CHURCH SERVICE SOCIETY. A Book of Common Order: Being Forms of Worship issued by the Church Service Society. Sixth Edition. [*In preparation.*

CLELAND. Barbara Allan, the Provost's Daughter. By ROBERT CLELAND, Author of 'Inchbracken,' 'True to a Type,' &c. 2 vols., 17s.

CLOUSTON. Popular Tales and Fictions: their Migrations and Transformations. By W. A. CLOUSTON, Editor of 'Arabian Poetry for English Readers,' 'The Book of Sindibad,' &c. 2 vols. post 8vo, roxburghe binding. 25s.

COBBAN. Master of his Fate. By J. MACLAREN COBBAN, Author of 'The Cure of Souls,' 'Tinted Vapours,' &c. Crown 8vo, 3s. 6d.

COCHRAN. A Handy Text-Book of Military Law. Compiled chiefly to assist Officers preparing for Examination; also for all Officers of the Regular and Auxiliary Forces. Comprising also a Synopsis of part of the Army Act. By Major F. COCHRAN, Hampshire Regiment Garrison Instructor, North British District. Crown 8vo, 7s. 6d.

COLQUHOUN. The Moor and the Loch. Containing Minute Instructions in all Highland Sports, with Wanderings over Crag and Corrie, Flood and Fell. By JOHN COLQUHOUN. Seventh Edition. With Illustrations. 8vo, 21s.

COTTERILL. Suggested Reforms in Public Schools. By C. C. COTTERILL, M.A., Assistant Master at Fettes College, Edin. Crown 8vo, 3s. 6d.

CRANSTOUN. The Elegies of Albius Tibullus. Translated into English Verse, with Life of the Poet, and Illustrative Notes. By JAMES CRANSTOUN, LL.D., Author of a Translation of 'Catullus.' Crown 8vo, 6s. 6d.

—— The Elegies of Sextus Propertius. Translated into English Verse, with Life of the Poet, and Illustrative Notes. Crown 8vo, 7s. 6d.

CRAWFORD. Saracinesca. By F. MARION CRAWFORD, Author of 'Mr Isaacs,' 'Dr Claudius,' 'Zoroaster,' &c. &c. Fourth Ed. Crown 8vo, 6s.

CRAWFORD. The Doctrine of Holy Scripture respecting the Atonement. By the late THOMAS J. CRAWFORD, D.D., Professor of Divinity in the University of Edinburgh. Fifth Edition. 8vo, 12s.

—— The Fatherhood of God, Considered in its General and Special Aspects, and particularly in relation to the Atonement, with a Review of Recent Speculations on the Subject. By the late THOMAS J. CRAWFORD, D.D., Professor of Divinity in the University of Edinburgh. Third Edition, Revised and Enlarged. 8vo, 9s.

—— The Preaching of the Cross, and other Sermons. 8vo, 7s. 6d.

—— The Mysteries of Christianity. Crown 8vo, 7s. 6d.

CRAWFORD. An Atonement of East London, and other Poems. By HOWARD CRAWFORD, M.A. Crown 8vo, 5s.

CUSHING. The Bull i' th' Thorn. A Romance. By PAUL CUSHING, Author of 'The Blacksmith of Voe,' &c. 3 vols. Crown 8vo, 25s. 6d.

DAVIES. Norfolk Broads and Rivers; or, The Waterways, Lagoons, and Decoys of East Anglia. By G. CHRISTOPHER DAVIES, Author of 'The Swan and her Crew.' Illustrated with Seven full-page Plates. New and Cheaper Edition. Crown 8vo, 6s.

———— Our Home in Aveyron. Sketches of Peasant Life in Aveyron and the Lot. By G. CHRISTOPHER DAVIES and Mrs BROUGHALL. Illustrated with full-page Illustrations. 8vo, 15s.

DAYNE. In the Name of the Tzar. A Novel. By J. BELFORD DAYNE. Crown 8vo, 6s.

———— Tribute to Satan. A Novel. Crown 8vo, 2s. 6d.

DE LA WARR. An Eastern Cruise in the 'Edeline.' By the Countess DE LA WARR. In Illustrated Cover. 2s.

DESCARTES. The Method, Meditations, and Principles of Philosophy of Descartes. Translated from the Original French and Latin. With a New Introductory Essay, Historical and Critical, on the Cartesian Philosophy. By JOHN VEITCH, LL.D., Professor of Logic and Rhetoric in the University of Glasgow. A New Edition, being the Ninth. Price 6s. 6d.

DICKSON. Gleanings from Japan. By W. G. DICKSON, Author of 'Japan: Being a Sketch of its History, Government, and Officers of the Empire.' With Illustrations. 8vo, 16s.

DOGS, OUR DOMESTICATED: Their Treatment in reference to Food, Diseases, Habits, Punishment, Accomplishments. By 'MAGENTA.' Crown 8vo, 2s. 6d.

DR HERMIONE. By the Author of 'Lady Bluebeard,' 'Zit and Xoe.' Crown 8vo, 6s.

DU CANE. The Odyssey of Homer, Books I.-XII. Translated into English Verse. By Sir CHARLES DU CANE, K.C.M.G. 8vo, 10s. 6d.

DUDGEON. History of the Edinburgh or Queen's Regiment Light Infantry Militia, now 3rd Battalion The Royal Scots; with an Account of the Origin and Progress of the Militia, and a Brief Sketch of the old Royal Scots. By Major R. C. DUDGEON, Adjutant 3rd Battalion The Royal Scots. Post 8vo, with Illustrations. 10s. 6d.

DUNCAN. Manual of the General Acts of Parliament relating to the Salmon Fisheries of Scotland from 1828 to 1882. By J. BARKER DUNCAN. Crown 8vo, 5s.

DUNSMORE. Manual of the Law of Scotland as to the Relations between Agricultural Tenants and their Landlords, Servants, Merchants, and Bowers. By W. DUNSMORE. 8vo, 7s. 6d.

DUPRE. Thoughts on Art, and Autobiographical Memoirs of Giovanni Dupré. Translated from the Italian by E. M. PERUZZI, with the permission of the Author. New Edition. With an Introduction by W. W. STORY. Crown 8vo, 10s. 6d.

ELIOT. George Eliot's Life, Related in her Letters and Journals. Arranged and Edited by her husband, J. W. CROSS. With Portrait and other Illustrations. Third Edition. 3 vols. post 8vo, 42s.

———— George Eliot's Life. (Cabinet Edition.) With Portrait and other Illustrations. 3 vols. crown 8vo, 15s.

———— George Eliot's Life. With Portrait and other Illustrations. New Edition, in one volume. Crown 8vo, 7s. 6d.

———— Works of George Eliot (Cabinet Edition). Handsomely printed in a new type, 21 volumes, crown 8vo, price £5, 5s. The Volumes are also sold separately, price 5s. each, viz.:—
Romola. 2 vols.—Silas Marner, The Lifted Veil, Brother Jacob. 1 vol.—Adam Bede. 2 vols.—Scenes of Clerical Life. 2 vols.—The Mill on the Floss. 2 vols.—Felix Holt. 2 vols.—Middlemarch. 3 vols.—Daniel Deronda. 3 vols.—The Spanish Gypsy. 1 vol.—Jubal, and other Poems, Old and New. 1 vol.—Theophrastus Such. 1 vol.—Essays. 1 vol.

ELIOT. Novels by GEORGE ELIOT. Cheap Edition. Adam Bede. Illustrated. 3s. 6d., cloth.—The Mill on the Floss. Illustrated. 3s. 6d., cloth.—Scenes of Clerical Life. Illustrated. 3s., cloth.—Silas Marner: the Weaver of Raveloe. Illustrated. 2s. 6d., cloth.—Felix Holt, the Radical. Illustrated. 3s. 6d., cloth.—Romola. With Vignette. 3s. 6d., cloth.

——— Middlemarch. Crown 8vo, 7s. 6d.

——— Daniel Deronda. Crown 8vo, 7s. 6d.

——— Essays. New Edition. Crown 8vo, 5s.

——— Impressions of Theophrastus Such. New Edition. Crown 8vo, 5s.

——— The Spanish Gypsy. New Edition. Crown 8vo, 5s.

——— The Legend of Jubal, and other Poems, Old and New. New Edition. Crown 8vo, 5s.

——— Wise, Witty, and Tender Sayings, in Prose and Verse. Selected from the Works of GEORGE ELIOT. Eighth Edition. Fcap. 8vo, 6s.

——— The George Eliot Birthday Book. Printed on fine paper, with red border, and handsomely bound in cloth, gilt. Fcap. 8vo, cloth, 3s. 6d. And in French morocco or Russia, 5s.

ESSAYS ON SOCIAL SUBJECTS. Originally published in the 'Saturday Review.' A New Edition. First and Second Series. 2 vols. crown 8vo, 6s. each.

EWALD. The Crown and its Advisers; or, Queen, Ministers, Lords and Commons. By ALEXANDER CHARLES EWALD, F.S.A. Crown 8vo, 5s.

FAITHS OF THE WORLD, The. A Concise History of the Great Religious Systems of the World. By various Authors. Being the St Giles' Lectures—Second Series. Crown 8vo, 5s.

FARRER. A Tour in Greece in 1880. By RICHARD RIDLEY FARRER. With Twenty-seven full-page Illustrations by LORD WINDSOR. Royal 8vo, with a Map, 21s.

FERRIER. Philosophical Works of the late James F. Ferrier, B.A. Oxon., Professor of Moral Philosophy and Political Economy, St Andrews. New Edition. Edited by Sir ALEX. GRANT, Bart., D.C.L., and Professor LUSHINGTON. 3 vols. crown 8vo, 34s. 6d.

——— Institutes of Metaphysic. Third Edition. 10s. 6d.

——— Lectures on the Early Greek Philosophy. Third Edition, 10s. 6d.

——— Philosophical Remains, including the Lectures on Early Greek Philosophy. 2 vols., 24s.

FLETCHER. Lectures on the Opening Clauses of the Litany delivered in St Paul's Church, Edinburgh. By JOHN B. FLETCHER, M.A. Crown 8vo, 4s.

FLINT. The Philosophy of History in Europe. By ROBERT FLINT, D.D., LL.D., Professor of Divinity, University of Edinburgh. 2 vols. 8vo. [New Edition in preparation.

——— Theism. Being the Baird Lecture for 1876. Seventh Edition. Crown 8vo, 7s. 6d.

——— Anti-Theistic Theories. Being the Baird Lecture for 1877. Fourth Edition. Crown 8vo, 10s. 6d.

——— Agnosticism. Being the Croall Lectures for 1887-88.
[In the press.

FORBES. Insulinde: Experiences of a Naturalist's Wife in the Eastern Archipelago. By Mrs H. O. FORBES. Post 8vo, with a Map. 8s. 6d.

FOREIGN CLASSICS FOR ENGLISH READERS. Edited by Mrs OLIPHANT. Price 2s. 6d. For List of Volumes published, see page 2.

FOTHERGILL. Diana Wentworth. By CAROLINE FOTHERGILL, Author of 'An Enthusiast,' &c. 3 vols. post 8vo, 25s. 6d.

FULLARTON. Merlin: A Dramatic Poem. By RALPH MACLEOD FULLARTON. Crown 8vo, 5s.

GALT. Annals of the Parish. By JOHN GALT. Fcap. 8vo, 2s.
—— The Provost. Fcap. 8vo, 2s.
—— Sir Andrew Wylie. Fcap. 8vo, 2s.
—— The Entail; or, The Laird of Grippy. Fcap. 8vo, 2s.

GENERAL ASSEMBLY OF THE CHURCH OF SCOTLAND.
—— Prayers for Social and Family Worship. Prepared by a Special Committee of the General Assembly of the Church of Scotland. Entirely New Edition, Revised and Enlarged. Fcap. 8vo, red edges, 2s.
—— Prayers for Family Worship. A Selection from the complete book. Fcap. 8vo, red edges, price 1s.
—— Scottish Hymnal, with Appendix Incorporated. Published for Use in Churches by Authority of the General Assembly. 1. Large type, cloth, red edges, 2s. 6d.; French morocco, 4s. 2. Bourgeois type, limp cloth, 1s.; French morocco, 2s. 3. Nonpareil type, cloth, red edges, 6d.; French morocco, 1s. 4d. 4. Paper covers, 3d. 5. Sunday-School Edition, paper covers, 1d. No. 1, bound with the Psalms and Paraphrases, French morocco, 8s. No. 2, bound with the Psalms and Paraphrases, cloth, 2s.; French morocco, 3s.

GERARD. Reata: What's in a Name. By E. D. GERARD. New Edition. Crown 8vo, 6s.
—— Beggar my Neighbour. New Edition. Crown 8vo, 6s.
—— The Waters of Hercules. New Edition. Crown 8vo, 6s.

GERARD. The Land beyond the Forest. Facts, Figures, and Fancies from Transylvania. By E. GERARD. In Two Volumes. With Maps and Illustrations. 25s.

GERARD. Lady Baby. By DOROTHEA GERARD, Author of 'Orthodox.' 3 vols. crown 8vo, 25s. 6d.

GERARD. Stonyhurst Latin Grammar. By Rev. JOHN GERARD. Fcap. 8vo, 3s.

GILL. Free Trade: an Inquiry into the Nature of its Operation. By RICHARD GILL. Crown 8vo, 7s. 6d.
—— Free Trade under Protection. Crown 8vo, 7s. 6d.

GOETHE'S FAUST. Translated into English Verse by Sir THEODORE MARTIN, K.C.B. Part I. Second Edition, post 8vo, 6s. Ninth Edition, fcap., 3s. 6d. Part II. Second Edition, revised. Fcap. 8vo, 6s.

GOETHE. Poems and Ballads of Goethe. Translated by Professor AYTOUN and Sir THEODORE MARTIN, K.C.B. Third Edition, fcap. 8vo, 6s.

GOODALL. Juxta Crucem. Studies of the Love that is over us. By the late Rev. CHARLES GOODALL, B.D., Minister of Barr. With a Memoir by Rev. Dr Strong, Glasgow, and Portrait. Crown 8vo, 6s.

GORDON CUMMING. At Home in Fiji. By C. F. GORDON CUMMING, Author of 'From the Hebrides to the Himalayas.' Fourth Edition, post 8vo. With Illustrations and Map. 7s. 6d.
—— A Lady's Cruise in a French Man-of-War. New and Cheaper Edition. 8vo. With Illustrations and Map. 12s. 6d.
—— Fire-Fountains. The Kingdom of Hawaii: Its Volcanoes, and the History of its Missions. With Map and Illustrations. 2 vols. 8vo, 25s.
—— Wanderings in China. New and Cheaper Edition. 8vo, with Illustrations, 10s.
—— Granite Crags: The Yō-semité Region of California. Illustrated with 8 Engravings. New and Cheaper Edition. 8vo, 8s. 6d.

GRAHAM. The Life and Work of Syed Ahmed Khan, C.S.I. By Lieut.-Colonel G. F. I. GRAHAM, B.S.C. 8vo, 14s.

GRANT. Bush-Life in Queensland. By A. C. GRANT. New Edition. Crown 8vo, 6s.

GRIFFITHS. Locked Up. By Major ARTHUR GRIFFITHS, Author of 'The Wrong Road,' 'Chronicles of Newgate,' &c. With Illustrations by C. J. STANILAND, R.I. Crown 8vo, 2s. 6d.

HAGGARD. Dodo and I. A Novel. By Captain ANDREW HAGGARD, D.S.O. Second Edition. Crown 8vo, 6s.

HALDANE. Subtropical Cultivations and Climates. A Handy Book for Planters, Colonists, and Settlers. By R. C. HALDANE. Post 8vo, 9s.

HALLETT. A Thousand Miles on an Elephant in the Shan States. By HOLT S. HALLETT, M. Inst. C.E., F.R.G.S., M.R.A.S., Hon. Member Manchester and Tyneside Geographical Societies. 8vo, with Maps and numerous Illustrations, 21s.

HAMERTON. Wenderholme: A Story of Lancashire and Yorkshire Life. By PHILIP GILBERT HAMERTON, Author of 'A Painter's Camp.' A New Edition. Crown 8vo, 6s.

HAMILTON. Lectures on Metaphysics. By Sir WILLIAM HAMILTON, Bart., Professor of Logic and Metaphysics in the University of Edinburgh. Edited by the Rev. H. L. MANSEL, B.D., LL.D., Dean of St Paul's; and JOHN VEITCH, M.A., Professor of Logic and Rhetoric, Glasgow. Seventh Edition. 2 vols. 8vo, 24s.

——— Lectures on Logic. Edited by the SAME. Third Edition. 2 vols., 24s.

——— Discussions on Philosophy and Literature, Education and University Reform. Third Edition, 8vo, 21s.

——— Memoir of Sir William Hamilton, Bart., Professor of Logic and Metaphysics in the University of Edinburgh. By Professor VEITCH, of the University of Glasgow. 8vo, with Portrait, 18s.

——— Sir William Hamilton: The Man and his Philosophy. Two Lectures delivered before the Edinburgh Philosophical Institution, January and February 1883. By the SAME. Crown 8vo, 2s.

HAMLEY. The Operations of War Explained and Illustrated. By Lieut.-General Sir EDWARD BRUCE HAMLEY, K.C.B., K.C.M.G., M.P. Fifth Edition, revised throughout. 4to, with numerous Illustrations, 30s.

——— National Defence; Articles and Speeches. Post 8vo, 6s.

——— Shakespeare's Funeral, and other Papers. Post 8vo, 7s. 6d.

——— Thomas Carlyle: An Essay. Second Edition. Crown 8vo. 2s. 6d.

——— On Outposts. Second Edition. 8vo, 2s.

——— Wellington's Career; A Military and Political Summary. Crown 8vo, 2s.

——— Lady Lee's Widowhood. Crown 8vo, 2s. 6d.

——— Our Poor Relations. A Philozoic Essay. With Illustrations, chiefly by Ernest Griset. Crown 8vo, cloth gilt, 3s. 6d.

HAMLEY. Guilty, or Not Guilty? A Tale. By Major-General W. G. HAMLEY, late of the Royal Engineers. New Edition. Crown 8vo, 3s. 6d.

HARRISON. The Scot in Ulster. The Story of the Scottish Settlement in Ulster. By JOHN HARRISON, Author of 'Oure Tounis Colledge.' Crown 8vo, 2s. 6d.

HASELL. Bible Partings. By E. J. HASELL. Crown 8vo, 6s.

——— Short Family Prayers. Cloth, 1s.

HAY. The Works of the Right Rev. Dr George Hay, Bishop of Edinburgh. Edited under the Supervision of the Right Rev. Bishop STRAIN. With Memoir and Portrait of the Author. 5 vols. crown 8vo, bound in extra cloth, £1, 1s. The following Volumes may be had separately—viz.:
The Devout Christian Instructed in the Law of Christ from the Written Word. 2 vols., 8s.—The Pious Christian Instructed in the Nature and Practice of the Principal Exercises of Piety. 1 vol., 4s.

HEATLEY. The Horse-Owner's Safeguard. A Handy Medical Guide for every Man who owns a Horse. By G. S. HEATLEY, M.R.C.V.S. Crown 8vo, 5s.

—— The Stock-Owner's Guide. A Handy Medical Treatise for every Man who owns an Ox or a Cow. Crown 8vo, 4s. 6d.

HEDDERWICK. Lays of Middle Age; and other Poems. By JAMES HEDDERWICK, LL.D. Price 3s. 6d.

HEMANS. The Poetical Works of Mrs Hemans. Copyright Editions.—One Volume, royal 8vo, 5s.—The Same, with Illustrations engraved on Steel, bound in cloth, gilt edges, 7s. 6d.—Six Volumes in Three, fcap., 12s. 6d. SELECT POEMS OF MRS HEMANS. Fcap., cloth, gilt edges, 3s.

HOME PRAYERS. By Ministers of the Church of Scotland and Members of the Church Service Society. Second Edition. Fcap. 8vo, 3s.

HOMER. The Odyssey. Translated into English Verse in the Spenserian Stanza. By PHILIP STANHOPE WORSLEY. Third Edition, 2 vols. fcap., 12s.

—— The Iliad. Translated by P. S. WORSLEY and Professor CONINGTON. 2 vols. crown 8vo, 21s.

HUTCHINSON. Hints on the Game of Golf. By HORACE G. HUTCHINSON. Fourth Edition. Fcap. 8vo, cloth, 1s. 6d.

IDDESLEIGH. Lectures and Essays. By the late EARL OF IDDESLEIGH, G.C.B., D.C.L., &c. 8vo, 16s.

INDEX GEOGRAPHICUS: Being a List, alphabetically arranged, of the Principal Places on the Globe, with the Countries and Subdivisions of the Countries in which they are situated, and their Latitudes and Longitudes. Applicable to all Modern Atlases and Maps. Imperial 8vo, pp. 676, 21s.

JAMIESON. Discussions on the Atonement: Is it Vicarious? By the Rev. GEORGE JAMIESON, A.M., B.D., D.D., Author of 'Profound Problems in Philosophy and Theology.' 8vo, 16s.

JEAN JAMBON. Our Trip to Blunderland; or, Grand Excursion to Blundertown and Back. By JEAN JAMBON. With Sixty Illustrations designed by CHARLES DOYLE, engraved by DALZIEL. Fourth Thousand. Cloth, gilt edges, 6s. 6d. Cheap Edition, cloth, 3s. 6d. Boards, 2s. 6d.

JENNINGS. Mr Gladstone: A Study. By LOUIS J. JENNINGS, M.P., Author of 'Republican Government in the United States,' 'The Croker Memoirs,' &c. Popular Edition. Crown 8vo, 1s.

JERNINGHAM. Reminiscences of an Attaché. By HUBERT E. H. JERNINGHAM. Second Edition. Crown 8vo, 5s.

—— Diane de Breteuille. A Love Story. Crown 8vo, 2s. 6d.

JOHNSTON. The Chemistry of Common Life. By Professor J. F. W. JOHNSTON. New Edition, Revised, and brought down to date. By ARTHUR HERBERT CHURCH, M.A. Oxon.; Author of 'Food: its Sources, Constituents, and Uses,' &c., &c. Illustrated with Maps and 102 Engravings on Wood. Complete in one volume, crown 8vo, 7s. 6d.

—— Elements of Agricultural Chemistry and Geology. Revised, and brought down to date. By Sir CHARLES A. CAMERON, M.D., F.R.C.S.I., &c. Fifteenth Edition. Fcap. 8vo, 6s. 6d.

JOHNSTON. Catechism of Agricultural Chemistry and Geology. An entirely New Edition, revised and enlarged, by Sir CHARLES A. CAMERON, M.D., F.R.C.S.I., &c. Eighty-sixth Thousand, with numerous Illustrations, 1s.

JOHNSTON. Patrick Hamilton: a Tragedy of the Reformation in Scotland, 1528. By T. P. JOHNSTON. Crown 8vo, with Two Etchings. 5s.

KENNEDY. Sport, Travel, and Adventures in Newfoundland and the West Indies. By Captain W. R. KENNEDY, R.N. With Illustrations by the Author. Post 8vo, 14s.

KER. Short Studies on St Paul's Letter to the Philippians. By Rev. WILLIAM LEE KER, Minister of Kilwinning. Crown 8vo, 5s.

KING. The Metamorphoses of Ovid. Translated in English Blank Verse. By HENRY KING, M.A., Fellow of Wadham College, Oxford, and of the Inner Temple, Barrister-at-Law. Crown 8vo, 10s. 6d.

KINGLAKE. History of the Invasion of the Crimea. By A. W. KINGLAKE. Cabinet Edition, revised. Illustrated with Maps and Plans. Complete in 9 Vols., crown 8vo, at 6s. each. The Vols. respectively contain: I. THE ORIGIN OF THE WAR. II. RUSSIA MET AND INVADED. III. THE BATTLE OF THE ALMA. IV. SEBASTOPOL AT BAY. V. THE BATTLE OF BALACLAVA. VI. THE BATTLE OF INKERMAN. VII. WINTER TROUBLES. VIII. and IX. FROM THE MORROW OF INKERMAN TO THE DEATH OF LORD RAGLAN. With an Index to the Complete Work.

———— History of the Invasion of the Crimea. Demy 8vo. Vol. VI. Winter Troubles. With a Map, 16s. Vols. VII. and VIII. From the Morrow of Inkerman to the Death of Lord Raglan. With an Index to the Whole Work. With Maps and Plans. 28s.

———— Eothen. A New Edition, uniform with the Cabinet Edition of the 'History of the Invasion of the Crimea,' price 6s.

KNOLLYS. The Elements of Field-Artillery. Designed for the Use of Infantry and Cavalry Officers. By HENRY KNOLLYS, Captain Royal Artillery; Author of 'From Sedan to Saarbrück,' Editor of 'Incidents in the Sepoy War,' &c. With Engravings. Crown 8vo, 7s. 6d.

LAWLESS. Hurrish: a Study. By the Hon. EMILY LAWLESS, Author of 'A Chelsea Householder,' &c. Fourth Edition, crown 8vo, 6s.

LEE. Glimpses in the Twilight. Being various Notes, Records, and Examples of the Supernatural. By the Rev. GEORGE F. LEE, D.C.L. Crown 8vo. 8s. 6d.

LEES. A Handbook of Sheriff Court Styles. By J. M. LEES, M.A., LL.B., Advocate, Sheriff-Substitute of Lanarkshire. New Ed., 8vo, 21s.

———— A Handbook of the Sheriff and Justice of Peace Small Debt Courts. 8vo, 7s. 6d.

LETTERS FROM THE HIGHLANDS. Reprinted from 'The Times.' Fcap. 8vo, 4s. 6d.

LIGHTFOOT. Studies in Philosophy. By the Rev. J. LIGHTFOOT, M.A., D.Sc., Vicar of Cross Stone, Todmorden. Crown 8vo, 4s. 6d.

LITTLE HAND AND MUCKLE GOLD. A Study of To-day. In 3 vols. post 8vo, 25s. 6d.

LOCKHART. Doubles and Quits. By LAURENCE W. M. LOCKHART. With Twelve Illustrations. Fourth Edition. Crown 8vo, 6s.

———— Fair to See: a Novel. Eighth Edition. Crown 8vo, 6s.

———— Mine is Thine: a Novel. Eighth Edition. Crown 8vo, 6s.

LORIMER. The Institutes of Law: A Treatise of the Principles of Jurisprudence as determined by Nature. By JAMES LORIMER, Regius Professor of Public Law and of the Law of Nature and Nations in the University of Edinburgh. New Edition, revised and much enlarged. 8vo, 18s.

LORIMER. The Institutes of the Law of Nations. A Treatise of the Jural Relation of Separate Political Communities. By JAMES LORIMER, Regius Professor of Public Law in the University of Edinburgh. In 2 vols. 8vo. Volume I., price 16s. Volume II., price 20s.

LYSTER. Another Such Victory! By ANNETTE LYSTER, Author of 'A Leal Light Heart,' 'Two Old Maids,' &c. 3 vols. crown 8vo, 25s. 6d.

M'COMBIE. Cattle and Cattle-Breeders. By WILLIAM M'COMBIE, Tillyfour. New Edition, enlarged, with Memoir of the Author. By JAMES MACDONALD, of the 'Farming World.' Crown 8vo, 3s. 6d.

MACRAE. A Handbook of Deer-Stalking. By ALEXANDER MACRAE, late Forester to Lord Henry Bentinck. With Introduction by HORATIO ROSS, Esq. Fcap. 8vo, with two Photographs from Life. 3s. 6d.

M'CRIE. Works of the Rev. Thomas M'Crie, D.D. Uniform Edition. Four vols. crown 8vo, 24s.

—— Life of John Knox. Containing Illustrations of the History of the Reformation in Scotland. Crown 8vo, 6s. Another Edition, 3s. 6d.

—— Life of Andrew Melville. Containing Illustrations of the Ecclesiastical and Literary History of Scotland in the Sixteenth and Seventeenth Centuries. Crown 8vo, 6s.

—— History of the Progress and Suppression of the Reformation in Italy in the Sixteenth Century. Crown 8vo, 4s.

—— History of the Progress and Suppression of the Reformation in Spain in the Sixteenth Century. Crown 8vo, 3s. 6d.

—— Lectures on the Book of Esther. Fcap. 8vo, 5s.

MACDONALD. A Manual of the Criminal Law (Scotland) Procedure Act, 1887. By NORMAN DORAN MACDONALD. Revised by the LORD JUSTICE-CLERK. 8vo, cloth. 10s. 6d.

MACGREGOR. Life and Opinions of Major-General Sir Charles MacGregor, K.C.B., C.S.I., C.I.E, Quartermaster-General of India. From his Letters and Diaries. Edited by LADY MACGREGOR. With Portraits and Maps to illustrate Campaigns in which he was engaged. 2 vols. 8vo, 35s.

M'INTOSH. The Book of the Garden. By CHARLES M'INTOSH, formerly Curator of the Royal Gardens of his Majesty the King of the Belgians, and lately of those of his Grace the Duke of Buccleuch, K.G., at Dalkeith Palace. 2 vols. royal 8vo, with 1350 Engravings. £4, 7s. 6d. Vol. I. On the Formation of Gardens and Construction of Garden Edifices. £2, 10s. Vol. II. Practical Gardening. £1, 17s. 6d.

MACINTYRE. Hindu-Koh: Wanderings and Wild Sports on and beyond the Himalayas. By Major-General DONALD MACINTYRE, V.C., late Prince of Wales' Own Goorkhas, F.R.G.S. Dedicated to H.R.H. The Prince of Wales. 8vo, with numerous Illustrations, 21s.

MACKAY. A Manual of Modern Geography; Mathematical, Physical, and Political. By the Rev. ALEXANDER MACKAY, LL.D., F.R.G.S. 11th Thousand, revised to the present time. Crown 8vo, pp. 688. 7s. 6d.

—— Elements of Modern Geography. 53d Thousand, revised to the present time. Crown 8vo, pp. 300, 3s.

—— The Intermediate Geography. By the Rev. ALEXANDER MACKAY, LL.D., F.R.G.S. Intended as an Intermediate Book between the Author's 'Outlines of Geography' and 'Elements of Geography.' Fifteenth Edition, revised. Crown 8vo, pp. 238, 2s.

—— Outlines of Modern Geography. 185th Thousand, revised to the present time. 18mo, pp. 118, 1s.

—— First Steps in Geography. 105th Thousand. 18mo, pp. 56. Sewed, 4d.; cloth, 6d.

—— Elements of Physiography and Physical Geography. With Express Reference to the Instructions recently issued by the Science and Art Department. 30th Thousand, revised. Crown 8vo, 1s. 6d.

—— Facts and Dates; or, the Leading Events in Sacred and Profane History, and the Principal Facts in the various Physical Sciences. The Memory being aided throughout by a Simple and Natural Method. For Schools and Private Reference. New Edition. Crown 8vo, 3s. 6d.

MACKAY. An Old Scots Brigade. Being the History of Mackay's Regiment, now incorporated with the Royal Scots. With an Appendix containing many Original Documents connected with the History of the Regiment. By JOHN MACKAY (late) OF HERRIESDALE. Crown 8vo, 5s.

MACKENZIE. Studies in Roman Law. With Comparative Views of the Laws of France, England, and Scotland. By LORD MACKENZIE, one of the Judges of the Court of Session in Scotland. Sixth Edition, Edited by JOHN KIRKPATRICK, Esq., M.A. Cantab.; Dr Jur. Heidelb.; LL.B. Edin.; Advocate. 8vo, 12s.

MAIN. Three Hundred English Sonnets. Chosen and Edited by DAVID M. MAIN. Fcap. 8vo, 6s.

MAIR. A Digest of Laws and Decisions, Ecclesiastical and Civil, relating to the Constitution, Practice, and Affairs of the Church of Scotland. With Notes and Forms of Procedure. By the Rev. WILLIAM MAIR, D.D., Minister of the Parish of Earlston. Crown 8vo. With Supplements, 8s.

MARMORNE. The Story is told by ADOLPHUS SEGRAVE, the youngest of three Brothers. Third Edition. Crown 8vo, 6s.

MARSHALL. French Home Life. By FREDERIC MARSHALL. Second Edition. 5s.

—— Claire Brandon. A Novel. 3 vols. crown 8vo, 25s. 6d.

MARSHMAN. History of India. From the Earliest Period to the Close of the India Company's Government; with an Epitome of Subsequent Events. By JOHN CLARK MARSHMAN, C.S.I. Abridged from the Author's larger work. Second Edition, revised. Crown 8vo, with Map, 6s. 6d.

MARTIN. Goethe's Faust. Part I. Translated by Sir THEODORE MARTIN, K.C.B. Second Ed., crown 8vo, 6s. Ninth Ed., fcap. 8vo, 3s. 6d.

—— Goethe's Faust. Part II. Translated into English Verse. Second Edition, revised. Fcap. 8vo, 6s.

—— The Works of Horace. Translated into English Verse, with Life and Notes. 2 vols. New Edition, crown 8vo, 21s.

—— Poems and Ballads of Heinrich Heine. Done into English Verse. Second Edition. Printed on *papier vergé*, crown 8vo, 8s.

—— The Song of the Bell, and other Translations from Schiller, Goethe, Uhland, and Others. Crown 8vo, 7s. 6d.

—— Catullus. With Life and Notes. Second Ed., post 8vo, 7s. 6d.

—— Aladdin: A Dramatic Poem. By ADAM OEHLENSCHLAEGER. Fcap. 8vo, 5s.

—— Correggio: A Tragedy. By OEHLENSCHLAEGER. With Notes. Fcap. 8vo, 3s.

—— King Rene's Daughter: A Danish Lyrical Drama. By HENRIK HERTZ. Second Edition, fcap., 2s. 6d.

MARTIN. On some of Shakespeare's Female Characters. In a Series of Letters. By HELENA FAUCIT, LADY MARTIN. Dedicated by permission to Her Most Gracious Majesty the Queen. Third Edition. 8vo, with Portrait, 7s. 6d.

MATHESON. Can the Old Faith Live with the New? or the Problem of Evolution and Revelation. By the Rev. GEORGE MATHESON, D.D. Third Edition. Crown 8vo, 7s. 6d.

—— The Psalmist and the Scientist; or, Modern Value of the Religious Sentiment. Crown 8vo, 7s. 6d.

—— Sacred Songs. Crown 8vo, 4s.

MAURICE. The Balance of Military Power in Europe. An Examination of the War Resources of Great Britain and the Continental States. By Colonel MAURICE, R.A., Professor of Military Art and History at the Royal Staff College. Crown 8vo, with a Map. 6s.

MICHEL. A Critical Inquiry into the Scottish Language. With the view of Illustrating the Rise and Progress of Civilisation in Scotland. By FRANCISQUE-MICHEL, F.S.A. Lond. and Scot., Correspondant de l'Institut de France, &c. 4to, printed on hand-made paper, and bound in Roxburghe, 66s.

MICHIE. The Larch: Being a Practical Treatise on its Culture and General Management. By CHRISTOPHER Y. MICHIE, Forester, Cullen House. Crown 8vo, with Illustrations. New and Cheaper Edition, enlarged, 5s.

—— The Practice of Forestry. Crown 8vo, with Illustrations. 6s.

MIDDLETON. The Story of Alastair Bhan Comyn; or, The Tragedy of Dunphail. A Tale of Tradition and Romance. By the Lady MIDDLETON. Square 8vo, 10s.

MILNE. The Problem of the Churchless and Poor in our Large Towns. With special reference to the Home Mission Work of the Church of Scotland. By the Rev. ROBT. MILNE, M.A., D.D., Ardler. Crown 8vo, 3s. 6d.

MINTO. A Manual of English Prose Literature, Biographical and Critical: designed mainly to show Characteristics of Style. By W. MINTO, M.A., Professor of Logic in the University of Aberdeen. Third Edition, revised. Crown 8vo, 7s. 6d.

—— Characteristics of English Poets, from Chaucer to Shirley. New Edition, revised. Crown 8vo, 7s. 6d.

MOIR. Life of Mansie Wauch, Tailor in Dalkeith. With 8 Illustrations on Steel, by the late GEORGE CRUIKSHANK. Crown 8vo, 3s. 6d. Another Edition, fcap. 8vo, 1s. 6d.

MOMERIE. Defects of Modern Christianity, and other Sermons. By ALFRED WILLIAMS MOMERIE, M.A., D.Sc., LL.D., Professor of Logic and Metaphysics in King's College, London. Third Edition. Crown 8vo, 5s.

—— The Basis of Religion. Being an Examination of Natural Religion. Second Edition. Crown 8vo, 2s. 6d.

—— The Origin of Evil, and other Sermons. Sixth Edition, enlarged. Crown 8vo, 5s.

—— Personality. The Beginning and End of Metaphysics, and a Necessary Assumption in all Positive Philosophy. Fourth Ed. Cr. 8vo, 3s.

—— Agnosticism. Second Edition, Revised. Crown 8vo, 5s.

—— Preaching and Hearing; and other Sermons. Second Edition. Crown 8vo, 4s. 6d.

—— Belief in God. Second Edition. Crown 8vo, 3s.

—— Inspiration; and other Sermons. Crown 8vo, 5s.

—— Church and Creed. Crown 8vo, 4s. 6d.

MONTAGUE. Campaigning in South Africa. Reminiscences of an Officer in 1879. By Captain W. E. MONTAGUE, 94th Regiment, Author of 'Claude Meadowleigh,' &c. 8vo, 10s. 6d.

MONTALEMBERT. Memoir of Count de Montalembert. A Chapter of Recent French History. By Mrs OLIPHANT, Author of the 'Life of Edward Irving,' &c. 2 vols. crown 8vo, £1, 4s.

MORISON. Sordello. An Outline Analysis of Mr Browning's Poem. By JEANIE MORISON, Author of 'The Purposes of the Ages,' 'Ane Booke of Ballades,' &c. Crown 8vo, 3s.

MUNRO. On Valuation of Property. By WILLIAM MUNRO, M.A., Her Majesty's Assessor of Railways and Canals for Scotland. Second Edition. Revised and enlarged. 8vo, 3s. 6d.

MURDOCH. Manual of the Law of Insolvency and Bankruptcy: Comprehending a Summary of the Law of Insolvency, Notour Bankruptcy, Composition-contracts, Trust-deeds, Cessios, and Sequestrations; and the Winding-up of Joint-Stock Companies in Scotland; with Annotations on the various Insolvency and Bankruptcy Statutes; and with Forms of Procedure applicable to these Subjects. By JAMES MURDOCH, Member of the Faculty of Procurators in Glasgow. Fifth Edition, Revised and Enlarged, 8vo, £1, 10s.

MY TRIVIAL LIFE AND MISFORTUNE: A Gossip with no Plot in Particular. By A PLAIN WOMAN. New Edition, crown 8vo, 6s.

By the SAME AUTHOR.

POOR NELLIE. New and Cheaper Edition. Crown 8vo, 6s.

NAPIER. The Construction of the Wonderful Canon of Logarithms (Mirifici Logarithmorum Canonis Constructio). By JOHN NAPIER of Merchiston. Translated for the first time, with Notes, and a Catalogue of Napier's Works, by WILLIAM RAE MACDONALD. Small 4to, 15s. *A few large paper copies may be had, printed on Whatman paper, price 30s.*

NEAVES. Songs and Verses, Social and Scientific. By an Old Contributor to 'Maga.' By the Hon. Lord NEAVES. Fifth Ed., fcap. 8vo, 4s.

—— The Greek Anthology. Being Vol. XX. of 'Ancient Classics for English Readers.' Crown 8vo, 2s. 6d.

NICHOLSON. A Manual of Zoology, for the Use of Students. With a General Introduction on the Principles of Zoology. By HENRY ALLEYNE NICHOLSON, M.D., D.Sc., F.L.S., F.G.S., Regius Professor of Natural History in the University of Aberdeen. Seventh Edition, rewritten and enlarged. Post 8vo, pp. 956, with 555 Engravings on Wood, 18s.

—— Text-Book of Zoology, for the Use of Schools. Fourth Edition, enlarged. Crown 8vo, with 188 Engravings on Wood, 7s. 6d.

—— Introductory Text-Book of Zoology, for the Use of Junior Classes. Sixth Edition, revised and enlarged, with 166 Engravings, 3s.

—— Outlines of Natural History, for Beginners; being Descriptions of a Progressive Series of Zoological Types. Third Edition, with Engravings, 1s. 6d.

—— A Manual of Palæontology, for the Use of Students. With a General Introduction on the Principles of Palæontology. By Professor H. ALLEYNE NICHOLSON and RICHARD LYDEKKER. Third Edition. Rewritten and greatly enlarged. 2 vols 8vo, with Engravings, £3, 3s.

—— The Ancient Life-History of the Earth. An Outline of the Principles and Leading Facts of Palæontological Science. Crown 8vo, with 276 Engravings, 10s. 6d.

—— On the "Tabulate Corals" of the Palæozoic Period, with Critical Descriptions of Illustrative Species. Illustrated with 15 Lithograph Plates and numerous Engravings. Super-royal 8vo, 21s.

—— Synopsis of the Classification of the Animal Kingdom. 8vo, with 106 Illustrations, 6s.

—— On the Structure and Affinities of the Genus Monticulipora and its Sub-Genera, with Critical Descriptions of Illustrative Species. Illustrated with numerous Engravings on wood and lithographed Plates. Super-royal 8vo, 18s.

NICHOLSON. Communion with Heaven, and other Sermons. By the late MAXWELL NICHOLSON, D.D., Minister of St Stephen's, Edinburgh. Crown 8vo, 5s. 6d.

—— Rest in Jesus. Sixth Edition. Fcap. 8vo, 4s. 6d.

NICHOLSON. A Treatise on Money, and Essays on Present Monetary Problems. By JOSEPH SHIELD NICHOLSON, M.A., D.Sc., Professor of Commercial and Political Economy and Mercantile Law in the University of Edinburgh. 8vo, 10s. 6d.

NICOLSON AND MURE. A Handbook to the Local Government (Scotland) Act, 1889. With Introduction, Explanatory Notes, and Index. By J. BADENACH NICOLSON, Advocate, Counsel to the Scotch Education Department, and W. J. MURE, Advocate, Legal Secretary to the Lord Advocate for Scotland. Ninth Reprint. 8vo, 5s.

OLIPHANT. Masollam: a Problem of the Period. A Novel. By LAURENCE OLIPHANT. 3 vols. post 8vo, 25s. 6d.

—— Scientific Religion; or, Higher Possibilities of Life and Practice through the Operation of Natural Forces. Second Edition. 8vo, 16s.

—— Altiora Peto. New and Cheaper Edition. Crown 8vo, boards, 2s. 6d. Illustrated Edition. Crown 8vo, cloth, 6s.

OLIPHANT. Piccadilly: A Fragment of Contemporary Biography. With Eight Illustrations by Richard Doyle. Eighth Edition, 4s. 6d. Cheap Edition, in paper cover. 2s. 6d.

—— Traits and Travesties; Social and Political. Post 8vo, 10s. 6d.

—— The Land of Gilead. With Excursions in the Lebanon. With Illustrations and Maps. Demy 8vo, 21s.

—— Haifa: Life in Modern Palestine. 2d Edition. 8vo, 7s. 6d.

—— Episodes in a Life of Adventure; or, Moss from a Rolling Stone. Fourth Edition. Post 8vo, 6s.

—— Fashionable Philosophy, and other Sketches. 1s.

OLIPHANT. Katie Stewart. By Mrs Oliphant. 2s. 6d.

—— The Duke's Daughter. A Novel. 3 vols. crown 8vo. [*Immediately.*

OSBORN. Narratives of Voyage and Adventure. By Admiral SHERARD OSBORN, C.B. 3 vols. crown 8vo, 12s.

OSSIAN. The Poems of Ossian in the Original Gaelic. With a Literal Translation into English, and a Dissertation on the Authenticity of the Poems. By the Rev. ARCHIBALD CLERK. 2 vols. imperial 8vo, £1, 11s. 6d.

OSWALD. By Fell and Fjord; or, Scenes and Studies in Iceland. By E. J. OSWALD. Post 8vo, with Illustrations. 7s. 6d.

OUTRAM. Lyrics: Legal and Miscellaneous. By the late GEORGE OUTRAM, Esq., Advocate. New Edition, with Explanatory Notes. Edited by J. H. Stoddart, LL.D.; and Illustrated by William Ralston and A. S. Boyd. Fcap. 8vo, 5s.

PAGE. Introductory Text-Book of Geology. By DAVID PAGE, LL.D., Professor of Geology in the Durham University of Physical Science, Newcastle, and Professor LAPWORTH of Mason Science College, Birmingham. With Engravings and Glossarial Index. Twelfth Edition. Revised and Enlarged. 3s. 6d.

—— Advanced Text-Book of Geology, Descriptive and Industrial. With Engravings, and Glossary of Scientific Terms. Sixth Edition, revised and enlarged, 7s. 6d.

—— Introductory Text-Book of Physical Geography. With Sketch-Maps and Illustrations. Edited by CHARLES LAPWORTH, LL.D., F.G.S., &c., Professor of Geology and Mineralogy in the Mason Science College, Birmingham. 12th Edition. 2s. 6d.

—— Advanced Text-Book of Physical Geography. Third Edition, Revised and Enlarged by Prof. LAPWORTH. With Engravings. 5s.

PATON. Spindrift. By Sir J. NOEL PATON. Fcap., cloth, 5s.

—— Poems by a Painter. Fcap., cloth, 5s.

PATON. Body and Soul. A Romance in Transcendental Pathology. By FREDERICK NOEL PATON. Third Edition. Crown 8vo, 1s.

PATTERSON. Essays in History and Art. By R. HOGARTH PATTERSON. 8vo, 12s.

—— The New Golden Age, and Influence of the Precious Metals upon the World. 2 vols. 8vo, 31s. 6d.

PAUL. History of the Royal Company of Archers, the Queen's Body-Guard for Scotland. By JAMES BALFOUR PAUL, Advocate of the Scottish Bar. Crown 4to, with Portraits and other Illustrations. £2, 2s.

PEILE. Lawn Tennis as a Game of Skill. With latest revised Laws as played by the Best Clubs. By Captain S. C. F. PEILE, B.S.C. Fourth Edition, fcap. cloth, 1s. 6d.

PETTIGREW. The Handy Book of Bees, and their Profitable Management. By A. PETTIGREW. Fifth Edition, Enlarged, with Engravings. Crown 8vo, 3s. 6d.

PHILOSOPHICAL CLASSICS FOR ENGLISH READERS.
Companion Series to Ancient and Foreign Classics for English Readers. Edited by WILLIAM KNIGHT, LL.D., Professor of Moral Philosophy, University of St Andrews. In crown 8vo volumes, with portraits, price 3s 6d.
[For list of Volumes published, see page 2.

POLLOK. The Course of Time : A Poem. By ROBERT POLLOK, A.M. Small fcap. 8vo, cloth gilt, 2s. 6d. The Cottage Edition, 32mo, sewed, 8d. The Same, cloth, gilt edges, 1s. 6d. Another Edition, with Illustrations by Birket Foster and others, fcap., gilt cloth, 3s. 6d., or with edges gilt, 4s.

PORT ROYAL LOGIC. Translated from the French ; with Introduction, Notes, and Appendix. By THOMAS SPENCER BAYNES, LL.D., Professor in the University of St Andrews. Tenth Edition, 12mo, 4s.

POTTS AND DARNELL. Aditus Faciliores : An easy Latin Construing Book, with Complete Vocabulary. By A. W. POTTS, M.A., LL.D., Head-Master of the Fettes College, Edinburgh: and the Rev. C. DARNELL, M.A., Head-Master of Cargilfield Preparatory School, Edinburgh. Tenth Edition, fcap. 8vo, 3s. 6d.

—— Aditus Faciliores Graeci. An easy Greek Construing Book, with Complete Vocabulary. Fourth Edition, fcap. 8vo, 3s.

PRINGLE. The Live-Stock of the Farm. By ROBERT O. PRINGLE. Third Edition. Revised and Edited by JAMES MACDONALD, of the 'Farming World,' &c. Crown 8vo, 7s. 6d.

PUBLIC GENERAL STATUTES AFFECTING SCOTLAND from 1707 to 1847, with Chronological Table and Index. 3 vols. large 8vo, £3, 3s.

PUBLIC GENERAL STATUTES AFFECTING SCOTLAND, COLLECTION OF. Published Annually with General Index.

RAMSAY. Rough Recollections of Military Service and Society. By Lieut.-Col. BALCARRES D. WARDLAW RAMSAY. Two vols. post 8vo, 21s.

RAMSAY. Scotland and Scotsmen in the Eighteenth Century. Edited from the MSS. of JOHN RAMSAY, Esq. of Ochtertyre, by ALEXANDER ALLARDYCE, Author of 'Memoir of Admiral Lord Keith, K.B.,' &c. 2 vols. 8vo. 31s. 6d.

RANKIN. A Handbook of the Church of Scotland. By JAMES RANKIN, D.D., Minister of Muthill; Author of 'Character Studies in the Old Testament,' &c. An entirely New and much Enlarged Edition. Crown 8vo, with 2 Maps, 7s. 6d.

RANKINE. A Treatise on the Rights and Burdens incident to the Ownership of Lands and other Heritages in Scotland. By JOHN RANKINE, M.A., Advocate, Professor of Scots Law in the University of Edinburgh. 8vo. *[New Edition in preparation.*

RECORDS OF THE TERCENTENARY FESTIVAL OF THE UNIVERSITY OF EDINBURGH. Celebrated in April 1884. Published under the Sanction of the Senatus Academicus. Large 4to, £2, 12s. 6d.

RICE. Reminiscences of Abraham Lincoln. By Distinguished Men of his Time. Collected and Edited by ALLEN THORNDIKE RICE, Editor of the 'North American Review.' Large 8vo, with Portraits, 21s.

ROBERTSON. Orellana, and other Poems. By J. LOGIE ROBERTSON, M.A. Fcap. 8vo. Printed on hand-made paper. 6s.

ROBERTSON. Our Holiday Among the Hills. By JAMES and JANET LOGIE ROBERTSON. Fcap. 8vo, 3s. 6d.

ROSCOE. Rambles with a Fishing-rod. By E. S. ROSCOE. Crown 8vo, 4s. 6d.

ROSS. Old Scottish Regimental Colours. By ANDREW ROSS, S.S.C., Hon. Secretary Old Scottish Regimental Colours Committee. Dedicated by Special Permission to Her Majesty the Queen. Folio. £2, 12s. 6d.

RUSSELL. The Haigs of Bemersyde. A Family History. By JOHN RUSSELL. Large 8vo, with Illustrations. 21s.

RUSSELL. Fragments from Many Tables. Being the Recollections of some Wise and Witty Men and Women. By GEO. RUSSELL. Cr. 8vo, 4s. 6d.

RUSSELL. Essays on Sacred Subjects for General Readers. By the Rev. WILLIAM RUSSELL, M.A. 8vo, 10s. 6d.

RUTLAND. Notes of an Irish Tour in 1846. By the DUKE OF RUTLAND, G.C.B. (Lord JOHN MANNERS). New Edition. Crown 8vo, 2s 6d.
——— Correspondence between the Right Honble. William Pitt and Charles Duke of Rutland, Lord Lieutenant of Ireland, 1781-1787. With Introductory Note by John Duke of Rutland. 8vo. [*Immediately.*
RUTLAND. Gems of German Poetry. Translated by the DUCHESS OF RUTLAND (Lady JOHN MANNERS). [*New Edition in preparation.*
——— Impressions of Bad-Homburg. Comprising a Short Account of the Women's Associations of Germany under the Red Cross. Crown 8vo, 1s. 6d.
——— Some Personal Recollections of the Later Years of the Earl of Beaconsfield, K.G. Sixth Edition, 6d.
——— Employment of Women in the Public Service. 6d.
——— Some of the Advantages of Easily Accessible Reading and Recreation Rooms, and Free Libraries. With Remarks on Starting and Maintaining Them. Second Edition, crown 8vo, 1s.
——— A Sequel to Rich Men's Dwellings, and other Occasional Papers. Crown 8vo, 2s. 6d.
——— Encouraging Experiences of Reading and Recreation Rooms, Aims of Guilds, Nottingham Social Guild, Existing Institutions, &c., &c. Crown 8vo, 1s.

SCHILLER. Wallenstein. A Dramatic Poem. By FREDERICK VON SCHILLER. Translated by C. G. A. LOCKHART. Fcap. 8vo, 7s. 6d.

SCOTCH LOCH FISHING. By "Black Palmer." Crown 8vo, interleaved with blank pages, 4s.

SCOUGAL. Scenes from a Silent World; or, Prisons and their Inmates. By FRANCIS SCOUGAL. Crown 8vo, 6s.

SELLAR. Manual of the Education Acts for Scotland. By the late ALEXANDER CRAIG SELLAR, M.P. Eighth Edition. Revised and in great part rewritten by J. EDWARD GRAHAM, B.A. Oxon., Advocate. Containing the Technical Schools Act, 1887, and all Acts bearing on Education in Scotland. With Rules for the conduct of Elections, with Notes and Cases. With a Supplement, being the Acts of 1889 in so far as affecting the Education Acts. 8vo, 12s. 6d.
[SUPPLEMENT TO SELLAR'S MANUAL OF THE EDUCATION ACTS FOR SCOTLAND. 8vo, 2s.]

SETH. Scottish Philosophy. A Comparison of the Scottish and German Answers to Hume. Balfour Philosophical Lectures, University of Edinburgh By ANDREW SETH, M.A., Professor of Logic, Rhetoric, and Metaphysics in St Andrews University. Second Edition. Crown 8vo, 5s.
——— Hegelianism and Personality. Balfour Philosophical Lectures. Second Series. Crown 8vo, 5s.

SETON. A Budget of Anecdotes. Chiefly relating to the Current Century. Compiled and Arranged by GEORGE SETON, Advocate, M.A. Oxon. New and Cheaper Edition, fcap. 8vo. Boards, 1s. 6d.

SHADWELL. The Life of Colin Campbell, Lord Clyde. Illustrated by Extracts from his Diary and Correspondence. By Lieutenant-General SHADWELL, C.B. 2 vols. 8vo. With Portrait, Maps, and Plans. 36s.

SHAND. Half a Century; or, Changes in Men and Manners. By ALEX. INNES SHAND, Author of 'Against Time,' &c. Second Ed., 8vo, 12s. 6d.
——— Letters from the West of Ireland. Reprinted from the 'Times.' Crown 8vo, 5s.

SHARPE. Letters from and to Charles Kirkpatrick Sharpe. Edited by ALEXANDER ALLARDYCE, Author of 'Memoir of Admiral Lord Keith, K.B.,' &c. With a Memoir by the Rev. W. K. R. BEDFORD. In two vols. 8vo. Illustrated with Etchings and other Engravings. £2, 12s. 6d.

SIM. Margaret Sim's Cookery. With an Introduction by L. B.
WALFORD, Author of 'Mr Smith: A Part of His Life.' &c. Crown 8vo, 5s.

SKELTON. Maitland of Lethington; and the Scotland of Mary
Stuart. A History. By JOHN SKELTON, C.B., LL.D., Author of 'The Essays of Shirley.' Demy 8vo. 2 vols., 28s.

——— The Local Government (Scotland) Act in Relation to Public
Health. A Handy Guide for County and District Councillors, Medical Officers, Sanitary Inspectors, and Members of Parochial Boards. Crown 8vo, 2s.

SMITH. Thorndale; or, The Conflict of Opinions. By WILLIAM
SMITH, Author of 'A Discourse on Ethics,' &c. New Edition. Cr. 8vo, 10s. 6d.

——— Gravenhurst; or, Thoughts on Good and Evil. Second
Edition, with Memoir of the Author. Crown 8vo, 8s.

——— The Story of William and Lucy Smith. Edited by
GEORGE MERRIAM. Large post 8vo, 12s. 6d.

SMITH. Memoir of the Families of M'Combie and Thoms,
originally M'Intosh and M'Thomas. Compiled from History and Tradition. By WILLIAM M'COMBIE SMITH. With Illustrations. 8vo.

SMITH. Greek Testament Lessons for Colleges, Schools, and
Private Students, consisting chiefly of the Sermon on the Mount and the Parables of our Lord. With Notes and Essays. By the Rev. J. HUNTER SMITH, M.A., King Edward's School, Birmingham. Crown 8vo, 6s.

SMITH. Writings by the Way. By JOHN CAMPBELL SMITH,
M.A., Sheriff-Substitute. Crown 8vo, 9s.

SMITH. The Secretary for Scotland. Being a Statement of the
Powers and Duties of the new Scottish Office. With a Short Historical Introduction and numerous references to important Administrative Documents. By W. C. SMITH, LL.B., Advocate. 8vo. 6s.

SOLTERA. A Lady's Ride Across Spanish Honduras. By MARIA
SOLTERA. With Illustrations. Post 8vo, 12s. 6d.

SORLEY. The Ethics of Naturalism. Being the Shaw Fellowship
Lectures, 1884. By W. R. SORLEY, M.A., Fellow of Trinity College, Cambridge, and Examiner in Philosophy in the University of Edinburgh. Crown 8vo, 6s.

SPEEDY. Sport in the Highlands and Lowlands of Scotland with
Rod and Gun. By TOM SPEEDY. Second Edition, Revised and Enlarged. With Illustrations by Lieut.-Gen. Hope Crealocke, C.B., C.M.G., and others. 8vo, 15s.

SPROTT. The Worship and Offices of the Church of Scotland.
By GEORGE W. SPROTT, D.D., Minister of North Berwick. Crown 8vo, 6s.

STAFFORD. How I Spent my Twentieth Year. Being a Record
of a Tour Round the World, 1886-87. By the MARCHIONESS OF STAFFORD. With Illustrations. Third Edition, crown 8vo, 8s. 6d.

STARFORTH. Villa Residences and Farm Architecture: A Series
of Designs. By JOHN STARFORTH, Architect. 102 Engravings. Second Edition, medium 4to, £2, 17s. 6d.

STATISTICAL ACCOUNT OF SCOTLAND. Complete, with
Index, 15 vols. 8vo, £16, 16s.
Each County sold separately, with Title, Index, and Map, neatly bound in cloth, forming a very valuable Manual to the Landowner, the Tenant, the Manufacturer, the Naturalist, the Tourist, &c

In course of publication.

STEPHENS' BOOK OF THE FARM; detailing the Labours of
the Farmer, Farm-Steward, Ploughman, Shepherd, Hedger, Farm-Labourer, Field-Worker, and Cattleman. Illustrated with numerous Portraits of Animals and Engravings of Implements. Fourth Edition. Revised, and in great part rewritten by JAMES MACDONALD, of the 'Farming World,' &c., &c. Assisted by many of the leading agricultural authorities of the day. To be completed in Six Divisional Volumes.
[*Divisions I. to IV., price* 10s. 6d. *each, now ready.*

STEPHENS. The Book of Farm Buildings; their Arrangement and Construction. By HENRY STEPHENS, F.R.S.E., Author of 'The Book of the Farm;' and ROBERT SCOTT BURN. Illustrated with 1045 Plates and Engravings. Large 8vo, uniform with 'The Book of the Farm,' &c. £1, 11s. 6d.

——— The Book of Farm Implements and Machines. By J. SLIGHT and R. SCOTT BURN, Engineers. Edited by HENRY STEPHENS. Large 8vo, uniform with 'The Book of the Farm,' £2, 2s.

STEVENSON. British Fungi. (Hymenomycetes.) By Rev. JOHN STEVENSON, Author of 'Mycologia Scotia,' Hon. Sec. Cryptogamic Society of Scotland. 2 vols. post 8vo, with Illustrations, price 12s. 6d. each.
Vol. I. AGARICUS—BOLBITIUS. Vol. II. CORTINARIUS—DACRYMYCES.

STEWART. Advice to Purchasers of Horses. By JOHN STEWART, V.S., Author of 'Stable Economy.' New Edition. 2s. 6d.

——— Stable Economy. A Treatise on the Management of Horses in relation to Stabling, Grooming, Feeding, Watering, and Working. By JOHN STEWART, V.S. Seventh Edition, fcap. 8vo, 6s 6d.

STODDART. Angling Songs. By THOMAS TOD STODDART. New Edition, with a Memoir by ANNA M. STODDART. Crown 8vo, 7s. 6d.

STORMONTH. Etymological and Pronouncing Dictionary of the English Language. Including a very Copious Selection of Scientific Terms. For Use in Schools and Colleges, and as a Book of General Reference. By the Rev. JAMES STORMONTH. The Pronunciation carefully Revised by the Rev. P. H. PHELP, M.A. Cantab. Tenth Edition, Revised throughout. Crown 8vo, pp. 800. 7s. 6d.

——— Dictionary of the English Language, Pronouncing, Etymological, and Explanatory. Revised by the Rev. P. H. PHELP. Library Edition. Imperial 8vo, handsomely bound in half morocco, 31s. 6d.

——— The School Etymological Dictionary and Word-Book. Fourth Edition. Fcap. 8vo, pp. 254. 2s.

STORY. Nero; A Historical Play. By W. W. STORY, Author of 'Roba di Roma.' Fcap. 8vo, 6s.

——— Vallombrosa. Post 8vo, 5s.

——— Poems. 2 vols. fcap., 7s. 6d.

——— Fiammetta. A Summer Idyl. Crown 8vo, 7s. 6d.

——— Conversations in a Studio. Crown 8vo. [*Immediately.*]

STRICKLAND. Life of Agnes Strickland. By her SISTER. Post 8vo, with Portrait engraved on Steel, 12s. 6d.

STURGIS. John-a-Dreams. A Tale. By JULIAN STURGIS. New Edition, crown 8vo, 3s. 6d.

——— Little Comedies, Old and New. Crown 8vo, 7s. 6d.

SUTHERLAND. Handbook of Hardy Herbaceous and Alpine Flowers, for general Garden Decoration. Containing Descriptions of upwards of 1000 Species of Ornamental Hardy Perennial and Alpine Plants; along with Concise and Plain Instructions for their Propagation and Culture. By WILLIAM SUTHERLAND, Landscape Gardener; formerly Manager of the Herbaceous Department at Kew. Crown 8vo, 7s. 6d.

TAYLOR. The Story of My Life. By the late Colonel MEADOWS TAYLOR, Author of 'The Confessions of a Thug,' &c. &c. Edited by his Daughter. New and cheaper Edition, being the Fourth. Crown 8vo, 6s.

THOLUCK. Hours of Christian Devotion. Translated from the German of A. Tholuck, D.D., Professor of Theology in the University of Halle. By the Rev. ROBERT MENZIES, D.D. With a Preface written for this Translation by the Author. Second Edition, crown 8vo, 7s. 6d.

THOMSON. Handy Book of the Flower-Garden: being Practical Directions for the Propagation, Culture, and Arrangement of Plants in Flower-Gardens all the year round. With Engraved Plans. By DAVID THOMSON, Gardener to his Grace the Duke of Buccleuch, K.T., at Drumlanrig. Fourth and Cheaper Edition, crown 8vo, 5s.

THOMSON. The Handy Book of Fruit-Culture under Glass: being a series of Elaborate Practical Treatises on the Cultivation and Forcing of Pines, Vines, Peaches, Figs, Melons, Strawberries, and Cucumbers. With Engravings of Hothouses, &c., most suitable for the Cultivation and Forcing of these Fruits. By DAVID THOMSON, Gardener to his Grace the Duke of Buccleuch, K.T., at Drumlanrig. Second Ed. Cr. 8vo, with Engravings, 7s. 6d.

THOMSON. A Practical Treatise on the Cultivation of the Grape Vine. By WILLIAM THOMSON, Tweed Vineyards. Tenth Edition, 8vo, 5s.

THOMSON. Cookery for the Sick and Convalescent. With Directions for the Preparation of Poultices, Fomentations, &c. By BARBARA THOMSON. Fcap. 8vo, 1s. 6d.

THOTH. A Romance. Third Edition. Crown 8vo, 4s. 6d.

By the Same Author.

A DREAMER OF DREAMS. A Modern Romance. Second Edition. Crown 8vo, 6s.

TOM CRINGLE'S LOG. A New Edition, with Illustrations. Crown 8vo, cloth gilt, 5s. Cheap Edition, 2s.

TRANSACTIONS OF THE HIGHLAND AND AGRICULTURAL SOCIETY OF SCOTLAND. Published annually, price 5s.

TULLOCH. Rational Theology and Christian Philosophy in England in the Seventeenth Century. By JOHN TULLOCH, D.D., Principal of St Mary's College in the University of St Andrews; and one of her Majesty's Chaplains in Ordinary in Scotland. Second Edition. 2 vols. 8vo, 16s.

—— Modern Theories in Philosophy and Religion. 8vo, 15s.

—— Luther, and other Leaders of the Reformation. Third Edition, enlarged. Crown 8vo, 3s. 6d.

—— Memoir of Principal Tulloch, D.D., LL.D. By Mrs OLIPHANT, Author of 'Life of Edward Irving.' Third and Cheaper Edition. 8vo, with Portrait. 7s. 6d.

TWO STORIES OF THE SEEN AND THE UNSEEN. 'THE OPEN DOOR,' 'OLD LADY MARY.' Crown 8vo, cloth, 2s. 6d.

VEITCH. Institutes of Logic. By JOHN VEITCH, LL.D., Professor of Logic and Rhetoric in the University of Glasgow. Post 8vo, 12s. 6d.

—— The Feeling for Nature in Scottish Poetry. From the Earliest Times to the Present Day. 2 vols. fcap. 8vo, in roxburghe binding. 15s.

—— Merlin and Other Poems. Fcap. 8vo. 4s. 6d.

—— Knowing and Being. Essays in Philosophy. First Series. Crown 8vo, 5s.

VIRGIL. The Æneid of Virgil. Translated in English Blank Verse by G. K. RICKARDS, M.A., and Lord RAVENSWORTH. 2 vols. fcap. 8vo, 10s.

WALFORD. A Stiff-Necked Generation. By L. B. WALFORD, Author of 'Mr Smith,' &c. Cheap Edition. Crown 8vo, 6s.

—— Four Biographies from 'Blackwood': Jane Taylor, Hannah More, Elizabeth Fry, Mary Somerville. Crown 8vo, 5s.

WARREN'S (SAMUEL) WORKS:—

Diary of a Late Physician. Cloth, 2s. 6d.; boards, 2s.

Ten Thousand A-Year. Cloth, 3s. 6d.; boards, 2s. 6d.

Now and Then. The Lily and the Bee. Intellectual and Moral Development of the Present Age. 4s. 6d.

Essays: Critical, Imaginative, and Juridical. 5s.

WARREN. The Five Books of the Psalms. With Marginal Notes. By Rev. SAMUEL L. WARREN, Rector of Esher, Surrey; late Fellow, Dean, and Divinity Lecturer, Wadham College, Oxford. Crown 8vo, 5s.

WEBSTER. The Angler and the Loop-Rod. By DAVID WEBSTER. Crown 8vo, with Illustrations, 7s. 6d.

WELLINGTON. Wellington Prize Essays on "the System of Field Manoeuvres best adapted for enabling our Troops to meet a Continental Army." Edited by Lieut.-General Sir EDWARD BRUCE HAMLEY, K.C.B. 8vo, 12s. 6d.

WENLEY. Socrates and Christ: A Study in the Philosophy of Religion. By R. M. WENLEY, M.A., Lecturer on Mental and Moral Philosophy in Queen Margaret College, Glasgow; Examiner in Philosophy in the University of Glasgow. Crown 8vo, 6s.

WERNER. A Visit to Stanley's Rear-Guard at Major Barttelot's Camp on the Aruhwimi. With an Account of River-Life on the Congo. By J. R. WERNER, F.R.G.S., Engineer, late in the Service of the Etat Indépendant du Congo. With Maps, Portraits, and other Illustrations. 8vo, 16s.

WESTMINSTER ASSEMBLY. Minutes of the Westminster Assembly, while engaged in preparing their Directory for Church Government, Confession of Faith, and Catechisms (November 1644 to March 1649). Edited by the Rev. Professor ALEX. T. MITCHELL, of St Andrews, and the Rev. JOHN STRUTHERS, LL.D. With a Historical and Critical Introduction by Professor Mitchell. 8vo, 15s.

WHITE. The Eighteen Christian Centuries. By the Rev. JAMES WHITE. Seventh Edition, post 8vo, with Index, 6s.

——— History of France, from the Earliest Times. Sixth Thousand, post 8vo, with Index, 6s.

WHITE. Archæological Sketches in Scotland—Kintyre and Knapdale. By Colonel T. P. WHITE, R.E., of the Ordnance Survey. With numerous Illustrations. 2 vols. folio, £4, 4s. Vol. I., Kintyre, sold separately, £2, 2s.

——— The Ordnance Survey of the United Kingdom. A Popular Account. Crown 8vo, 5s.

WILLIAMSON. Poems of Nature and Life. By DAVID R. WILLIAMSON, Minister of Kirkmaiden. Fcap. 8vo, 3s.

WILLS AND GREENE. Drawing-room Dramas for Children. By W. G. WILLS and the Hon. Mrs GREENE. Crown 8vo, 6s.

WILSON. Works of Professor Wilson. Edited by his Son-in-Law Professor FERRIER. 12 vols. crown 8vo, £2, 8s.

——— Christopher in his Sporting-Jacket. 2 vols., 8s.

——— Isle of Palms, City of the Plague, and other Poems. 4s.

——— Lights and Shadows of Scottish Life, and other Tales. 4s.

——— Essays, Critical and Imaginative. 4 vols., 16s.

——— The Noctes Ambrosianæ. 4 vols., 16s.

——— Homer and his Translators, and the Greek Drama. Crown 8vo, 4s.

WINGATE. Lily Neil. A Poem. By DAVID WINGATE. Crown 8vo, 4s. 6d.

WORDSWORTH. The Historical Plays of Shakspeare. With Introductions and Notes. By CHARLES WORDSWORTH, D.C.L., Bishop of S. Andrews. 3 vols. post 8vo, each price 7s. 6d.

WORSLEY. Poems and Translations. By PHILIP STANHOPE WORSLEY, M.A. Edited by EDWARD WORSLEY. Second Edition, enlarged. Fcap. 8vo, 6s.

YATE. England and Russia Face to Face in Asia. A Record of Travel with the Afghan Boundary Commission. By Captain A. C. YATE, Bombay Staff Corps. 8vo, with Maps and Illustrations, 21s.

YATE. Northern Afghanistan; or, Letters from the Afghan Boundary Commission. By Major C. E. YATE, C.S.I., C.M.G. Bombay Staff Corps, F.R.G.S. 8vo, with Maps. 18s.

YOUNG. A Story of Active Service in Foreign Lands. Compiled from letters sent home from South Africa, India, and China, 1856-1882. By Surgeon-General A. GRAHAM YOUNG, Author of 'Crimean Cracks.' Crown 8vo, Illustrated, 7s. 6d.

YULE. Fortification: for the Use of Officers in the Army, and Readers of Military History. By Col. YULE, Bengal Engineers. 8vo, with numerous Illustrations, 10s. 6d.

www.ingramcontent.com/pod-product-compliance
Lightning Source LLC
Chambersburg PA
CBHW032045230426
43672CB00009B/1483